I Hate To Read

My Complicated Love Story With Reading

I Hate To Read

My Complicated Love Story With Reading

Aaron M. Arrowood

Woodsong Publishing
Seymour, IN

WOODSONG
P U B L I S H I N G

I Hate To Read

My Complicated Love Story With Reading

Aaron M. Arrowood

Woodsong Publishing
5989 Spring Meadow Lane
Seymour, IN 47274

You may purchase an additional book, Countercultural Youth Ministries, written by Aaron Arrowood, from the Woodsong Publishing website or through your preferred booksellers.

www.woodsongpublishing.com
woodsongpublishing@yahoo.com

Cover design by Vision Graphics, Seymour, IN

Printed in the United States of America

ISBN 978-1-7349323-5-5

Table of Contents

Chapter 1	Why "I Hate To Read"	7
Chapter 2	The Problem: Ignorance	17
Chapter 3	The Solution: Reading	27
Chapter 4	There Are No Substitutes	39
Chapter 5	Reading Books: The Best Way To Learn	53
Chapter 6	You Can Love Reading	69
Chapter 7	How To Find A Good Book	73
Chapter 8	Finding Your Long-term Motivation	81
Chapter 9	Expanding Your Appetite	87
Chapter 10	Audiobook Workaround	93
Chapter 11	Plot Your Course And Track Your Progress	99
Chapter 12	Reading Something Old	103
Chapter 13	Connect The Dots	107
Chapter 14	My Book Recommendations	113
Conclusion		130

CHAPTER ONE
Why "I Hate To Read"

Thank you for buying, borrowing, or stumbling upon this book. If you acquired it because of the title, thank you for now trying to read it. If you desire to read and know that you should read but find it incredibly difficult to do so, this is the right book for you. I've walked in your shoes but don't worry, athlete's foot is only "mildly" contagious. However, we probably have a similar case of a rare disorder: *readerititus* I think that's a Latin word for an aversion to reading, though I can't say for sure, because I never finished my Latin textbook. Full confession: I've spent the majority of my life complaining, "I hate reading."

Here are the top nine things I always hated about reading:

1. You're expected to sit still while you read. You learn to read in school, and everybody knows you're supposed to sit still at school. The main problem with sitting still is that you're not moving around. Being still is what you do when you're trying to sleep, which is one of the reactions I have had from reading. It was like my body sensed the lack of motion and

automatically went into standby. Everybody knows that computers don't work in standby mode unless you have malware. In which case your computer is videoing you, sending porn to everybody in your contacts, or using your PayPal account.

2. Staring at paper is boring. Paper is inanimate. It just sits there doing nothing. Whoever had the idea of recording such important stuff on a medium as mundane as paper should be beaten.

3. My eyes won't go to the right line. I've always skipped steps while going up a flight of stairs. That's how I read—skipping about every other line. I go all out trying to get my eyes to proceed to the correct next line, but it's so hard. They skip up a line, or they jump two lines down. It's like a bad game of Mother May I.

4. Concentrating on one thing can be monotonous. There are literally millions of amazing things I could be thinking about instead of whatever "boring" stuff I'm reading. I could be contemplating lunch options, methods to help my co-worker stop munching ice, or ways to avoid reading. Generally, at least a million or so of those great options come to me before I get

through the first page.

5. Nerds read. What I learned in school—while I wasn't reading—is that cool guys skulk around ogling females while geeks sit and read. There was one Indian boy in my small grade school. You never saw him without a book in his hands or a mustard stain on his pants. I bet he's still reading in between managing half the hotels in the Midwest. What a dork!

6. Reading challenges paradigms and habits. I get pretty tired of having experts tell me how to live my life. If I want to eat poorly, burn bridges, or stagnate in my career, that's my prerogative. No, thank you, Dave Ramsey. Maybe I don't want to have financial freedom. Not everybody is cut from the same cloth. I'm marching to a different drummer. Perhaps you think its "humdrum," but I'm content.

7. Reading doesn't pay. Literally, no one will pay you to read.

8. Reading makes me hurt. It makes my eyes hurt. It makes my head hurt. It makes my back hurt. While I'm reading, I can think of dozens of things that hurt that I don't ever remember

hurting before I picked up a book.

9. It's hard to do other things. It's super challenging to get things done while reading. You can't peruse your email, watch satisfying videos on YouTube, or listen to the political pundits rant about current political stuff that you can't do anything about. Just think about what you might be missing while you're wasting your time reading. That Nigerian prince might get someone else to wire him the cash, and he'll release all that money to them. You gotta think through these things.

I'll never forget the look of dismay on my professor's face when I answered his question, "What books are you reading for inspiration?" I said, "I don't read books. My inspiration comes from my head."

Yep! That came out of my mouth in a college class. Nope! It wasn't some absurd and humiliating dream. I was fully clothed when I said it, but my bare ignorance was on display for all to see. My statement sounded to me like rock-solid proof of my unimpeachable intelligence. Thankfully, today, I understand it to prove something entirely different.

If I said it once, I said it a thousand times: "I hate reading." From grade school into adulthood, I always hated reading. I hated to read instructions. I hated to read articles. I hated to read magazines. I hated to read the newspaper. Most of all, I hated to read books. Although, to be honest, it's hard to say I hated to read books because, as they say, "you can't knock it 'til you've tried it."

When I was about seven years old, my dad offered to pay me for each book I read. I remember going to the library and finding the shortest books with the most pictures. *The Monster at the End of this Book* remained one of my most significant literary endeavors well beyond college and deep into adulthood.

Don't judge me. There's a reason you bought this book. Maybe you bought the book for a friend who is struggling in college or his career. Your friend feels stagnant and uninspired. More likely, you are like I was, and you need a swift kick. Whether you're reading this book for yourself or a friend, I want you to know that there is hope for you, or rather, for them.

Here's the thing: it's not just that I wanted to be a bibliophobe. I truly had what I can only describe as a physical reaction to reading. I could walk into the library: so far, so good. I could search through the available stacks with no problem. Hundreds of titles and subjects piqued my interest. I could easily find a book that sounded great, pick a comfy place to sit, prop up my feet, and even open the book to page one with no problem. Through paragraph one I would do okay. Halfway through paragraph two, I started to sweat. Then my head started swimming, heart began racing, and the walls would soon close in. As my eyes attempted to make the leaps from the end of one line to the beginning of the next, they repeatedly skipped to the wrong line. The slow reading made me want to scream. Anger began to set in. Ultimately, I hated whatever book I was reading more than anything in the world. If only I could go outside, breathe fresh air, move around—not read. Even now, sitting here trying to write this paragraph is bringing back a lot of bad memories; I can feel my restless legs beginning to get antsy.

Anytime I wasn't seized with a sudden bout of reading-induced narcolepsy, the preceding description is pretty much how I felt every time I tried to read anything. So, call it a cover story, call it insecurity, call it whatever you want; I called it, "I hate reading!"

In high school and college I felt like Muggsy Bogues in a room of Manute Bols: always having to run faster and jump higher to compensate for the fact that I wasn't reading ANYTHING. I can't imagine how much easier it would have been to write research papers if I would have read ANY of my references. To say my written work was a snow job is an understatement. Every time I wrote a paper, I was producing artificial snow in July in Florida. Do you know how hard it is to do that? My guess, since you're reading this book, is that you do. If it wasn't for my mother, and then my wife, I never would have graduated from college.

After college I took a job as a youth director: speaking to young minds at least once a week. The wellspring of inspiration that I referenced on that fateful day in college held out for exactly thirteen minutes. I'm kidding; fortunately, it held out for at least fourteen minutes. No. No. I'm going to establish right now that this book is about truth. It only lasted eleven minutes. My mental aquifer turned out to be a puddle. Imagine that a pig steps in the sand on a hot day, and the sweat from his little porky legs drips into his hoofprint. I know that pigs don't sweat. That is part of the point. Stop judging me and imagine that there was such a thing as pig sweat, and it fills that little tiny pig-foot hole. That is how much inspiration I had. And after three or four lectures, the well went dry.

I would be thrilled to tell you that as soon as my great ideas ran out, I immediately sought sources of fresh material. That would be below the level of honesty to which I have already committed myself. There is a single bright spot in this sad narrative of the first half of my twenty years in public speaking: none of my inspirational talks were recorded. Maybe I'm overly self-effacing. I guess you'll never know.

There is some good news for me and maybe for you. Even though I was almost proud of the fact that I hated to read and that reading was nearly a physical impossibility for me, today there are few things I love more than reading a book. I love short books and long books, fiction and non-fiction, classics and books that are hot-off-the-press, history, philosophy, biography, individual books, and series. I read early in the morning, throughout the day, and at night in bed. I read for entertainment, relaxation, and inspiration. I read because I want to. I read to learn. I read for pleasure. It's a pastime, a hobby, a passion, and a goal. Sometimes I discipline myself to read some particular thing, other times I have to force myself to stop reading. Far from the bumbling, blockheaded, book hater that I once was, today I have become a much more self-aware blockhead that loves reading more than any activity besides family, friends, and spiritual endeavors.

In this short book, I want to tell you my love story with reading. It's not a complete story, for I'm somewhere in the first chapters of my experience. I feel far behind where I should be. I wish that I would have fallen in love with books when I was thirteen instead of thirty-five. My hope is that the story of my metamorphosis might inspire someone in grade school, or high school—or any age—to embark on a journey of reading. Maybe my account comes at a critical time in your college years, and you'll make the commitment to truly read the texts. Maybe you're later on in life. Now is the best time to start. If you develop a relationship with books, I promise you this: reading will shape your thoughts, sharpen your mind, inspire, convict, challenge, and change you like nothing short of a supernatural, Moses-like encounter. My sincere hope is that this will be the last book that you hate to read.

If I could only give my kids two things in life, one of those things would be a love for reading. If I leave them money, they might become spendthrifts, lazy, or worse, fall in love with it. If I bequeath land, they might turn it into a landfill. If I teach them work-ethics, they might use that knowledge to climb the ladder of success, stepping on people all the way to the top. They might become insurance tycoons that milk senior citizens for their lifelong savings.

If I help my kids to fall in love with reading, they might still choose to be lazy or greedy or become slumlords, but, at least, they'll be doing it with full awareness. If they will read, they will encounter—face to face—great people and high ideas. While being exposed to virtue, valor, and genius, it will be difficult for them to live at peace with their own deficiencies. There is a good chance they will rise to the level of their influences.

I understand all the reasons not to read. I made my own justifications for years. Some of them are legitimate. Nevertheless, there are many more surpassingly warranted reasons in favor of reading. In this book, I will attempt to identify the benefits of reading as well as the concerns that I have for non-readers. This book is a simple strategy to becoming an avid reader. No matter how you feel about reading today, I am ninety-eight percent sure you will have your own love affair with reading. When you do, you will be forever changed and perpetually growing.

CHAPTER TWO
The Problem: Ignorance

Ignorance can be dangerous. Ignorant bomb diffusers, surgeons, and air traffic controllers can cause real problems. Uninformed voters are liable to elect corrupt politicians, and so forth. However, I don't want to address issues that ignorant people cause for society. I want to talk about how adversely ignorance can hurt you or me.

Ignorance is a real handicap. It's like walking around all day unaware of a "Kick Me!" sticker that's taped to your backside. People are laughing, and you have no idea why.

I'm reminded of the time I was doing some video production work for a college in Michigan. While brainstorming with several faculty members, a man walked into the room and sat right in the middle of the group. Since he looked like the janitor, I assumed he was the janitor. Unbelievably, he started interjecting ideas into the conversation. You can only imagine how irritating it was for me to have the janitor piping up in the middle of my brilliant brainstorming session. I don't know how much of my contempt was evident on my face, but I recall that I didn't ask, "Why don't you shut up and go clean something?" However, I imagine the faculty of that college is still laughing at me for wrongfully assuming that the president of the school was an idiot. He was not an idiot. He is known all over the world in his particular field. He has been a part of presidential panels discussing things I can't even pronounce. I am confident that he had a lot of good input. However, I was so busy hearing myself talk that I did not perceive it.

This is standard stuff. Imagine that there are four people in a room: an idiot, a novice, a dedicated student, and a wise man. The conversation might go something like this:

Idiot: "I'm goin' tell ya'll somethin; dogs is man's bess friends."

Novice: "Really? How do you know?"

Idiot: "Jus think about it; Benji, Lassie, Scoobie-doo, Rin-tin-tin, Toto, Air-Buddy. You know what they got? Loyalty. They ain't like people that jus does whatever."

Novice: "Dude! Those are all TV dogs, and those aren't those dogs' real names."

Idiot: "You think I don't know that? Everybody on TV's got a fake name. But they wouldn't of taken those parts if they didn't believe in what they was doing."

Novice: "You are so stupid. Dogs don't decide what

movies they will be in or what parts they'll take. Their owners make those decisions. And, by the way, Scoobie-doo is a cartoon character."

Idiot: "I know that. But, they still has to have a dog to do the voice parts."

Dedicated student: "Guys, guys! According to Wikipedia, 'Man's best friend' is a common phrase about domestic dogs, referring to their millennia-long history of close relations, loyalty, and companionship with humans."

Novice: "I'm sorry to contradict you, but I saw on Facebook the other day that dogs turn on people all the time. Like fifty percent of dogs, or five percent, or something will turn on their owners. It's pretty scary."

Idiot: "If fifty dogs has turned on their owners, then that would be all over the news."

Dedicated student: (Directing his question to the wise man) "Do you think dogs are man's best friend?"

Wise Man: "Some are."

How many times have you unwillingly listened to a lecture on politics, the fairness/unfairness of an employer, child-rearing, and the like by the least qualified person in the room? All the while, the real brainiac in the place sits quietly?

An idiot believes he knows it all and proudly attempts to illustrate as much. A stagnant mind produces an ocean of words. Avoid this level of ignorance at all costs.

For the novice, knowledge slows speaking, but impulsive words flow from a trickle of information. Indulge the ramblings of the partially educated at your own risk.

For the dedicated student, learning and talking must eventually come to a draw. A stream of words will flow from a stream of information. There's hope for the one who can listen as much as they talk.

For the wise man, reading, listening, and a desire to know stanches a desire to monologue. A trickle of words flows from a river of information. Don't mistake silence for ignorance, acquiescence, or approval. If you want the opinion of a learner, you may have to solicit it.

I've observed the wise. I envy their capacity to learn and their propensity to forbear. Sparse words fitly spoken flow from an ocean of information. If an erudite person speaks, wise men listen.

Often, ignorance and confidence go hand-in-hand. Imagine a

man who spends his entire life out in the middle of a cornfield. For this metaphor to work, it has to be a cornfield that never gets harvested. Also, the story assumes that the guy out in the middle of the cornfield can subsist on corn alone, without shelter, water, love, etc. With those preordained necessities, let's get back to the story…. The man has spent years living in a few square feet surrounded by nine-foot tall stalks of corn. He knows almost nothing about the world at large, but at the same time, he knows absolutely everything about his tiny corn patch. He knows everything about the dirt. He knows everything about the few bugs that occupy his space. He knows everything about the perpetual cornstalks. Just ask him! He knows everything there is to know about the world about which he is aware.

That guy was me—minus the strange existence in the middle of a perpetual cornfield. I was living in a proverbial cornfield of my own making. I knew so little, and yet I just knew that I knew so much. Ignorance and confidence go together like ammonium nitrate and aluminum, and they're just as explosive as Tannerite to your reputation and success.

Imagine that the guy out in the cornfield gets his hands on a step stool. If he can climb just a little bit higher, he'll see so much more. What if he acquires a six-foot ladder? Infrequently, I use a twenty-five-foot step ladder. Imagine that behemoth sitting in the middle of a cornfield. Each rung of the ladder simultaneously brings knowledge and humility. First, it exposes the man to information—there's a lot more corn than he realized; the field is so large. Beyond the field are trees, fence rows, power lines, houses, roads, and cars. All of that information is fascinating and thrilling but also humbling. With each new piece of information comes the realization of how little he knew and how limited is his knowledge about the things of which he is now aware. A lifetime of climbing will broaden the spectrum of experience, but it should also enforce a stunned silence that gazes in awe upon a world about which he knows so little.

For me, "I hate to read" was code for, "don't listen to whatever is getting ready to come out of my mouth." It meant that I didn't have any idea what I was talking about or that my knowledge would be about a few things I thought about constantly.

I should say, not everyone that reads is wise, and not everyone that hates reading is an idiot. For instance, not everyone in Oakland hates Jose Conseco. Oh, wait! Kidding aside, I've met bookworms that challenge the premise of this book. Conversely, I've known people who don't read but have great wisdom. It's not impossible to be smart without reading; it's just much harder. Some people are extremely gifted with knowledge and / or wisdom. The problem is that some people will read this book and think that describes them. If you think your giftings are off the chart, well, I think I've already described you in this chapter.

Not only do my original thoughts tend to fall in the ignorance-spectrum, but they also seem to lean towards negativity, fear, jealousy, anger, and pride. Simply put, my brain left to itself doesn't do me or anyone else a whole lot of good. It's a fact that your mind doesn't have marrow to produce fresh thoughts or kidneys to filter the old ones. Reading can be the remedy. It infuses brand new material into the cognitive stream and does dialysis on what's already there.

Our lives can become very repetitive. Wake up, make the bed. Make some breakfast, check the weather, eat the breakfast. Take a shower, throw on some clothes, climb into your car. Push the garage door button, tune the radio, check the rearview mirror, and drive on the same road you drove on yesterday, the day before that, the day before that, and day before that. Show up at work, clock in, do your job. Take a lunch break, check your phone messages. Finish your shift, clock out, drive home. Turn on the TV, eat dinner, get undressed, go to bed. While drifting off to sleep, think about tomorrow, set the alarm, wake up, etc. And, if you are anything like me, you are considering the same thoughts you've had one million times before while doing the same segment of your daily routine.

"There I go again. I always start shaving on the same side of my face. I wonder why?"

"I wish my wife would iron all of my clothes so I can wear whatever I want. Maybe I should iron my clothes. I'm hungry."

"Women drivers!"

"I can't believe that guy just pulled out in front of me. I hate that guy. And there it is; he's got a Christian radio station bumper sticker. Typical."

"I'll go this way because this route will shave thirty seconds off my ETA. Brilliant. My wife always goes the wrong way. Women!"

"Why is this building always 65°? How much would it cost them to make our workplace comfortable? Bosses!"

Those are just a few of the brilliant musings I ponder every day.

If we are not careful, we will become experts on minutia. We can become the trusted resource on all things irrelevant. We can become deeply convinced of ideas just because we've thought them a thousand times. We're in danger of becoming self-assured, steeped in our own opinions; self-centered, focused on our own desires; inflexible, not necessarily in love with our routine but so familiar with it that we can't imagine life any other way.

Reading expands knowledge, and knowledge can break you out of your routines, your habitual thoughts, and your self-centric lifestyle. Knowledge brings empathy; further, it inspires love, it challenges us to grow, sometimes makes us angry, forces us to find solutions or resolution, and gives us hope. Knowledge causes us to become disenchanted with what is and more inclined to dream.

Ignorance is a condition that thrives in mental isolation. Reading is the cure. In the next chapter we will discuss the power of knowledge.

CHAPTER THREE
The Solution: Reading Books

Sir Francis Bacon in *Meditationes Sacrae and Human Philosophy* said, "Knowledge is power." In this chapter, I want to share three dominant characteristics that are the result of knowledge through reading.

Knowledge can make you qualified

First, knowledge prepares you to do things well. Knowledge can make you an engaging friend, a valuable employee, an inspiring leader, a firm believer, a great citizen, and a worthy Christian. Pick just about anything at which you'd like to be proficient, and the chances are good that your local public library has several volumes that will help you. They are available for free.

I have often been induced to accept some worthless promotional trinket because it was free. I have a drawer at my house full of logoed items: pens and key chain flashlights, tiny knives. I accepted them, not because I needed them, but because I didn't have to pay for them. Sitting on shelves in your local library are thousands of books containing valuable information on just about every subject known to man. This extraordinary resource is available to anyone for free.

Why should you take that mug? It's right there. It's free. Take one. Why should you take advantage of the millions of books that are available? Why should you become proficient in or knowledgeable of any range of skills or subjects? Because you can.

Learn a foreign language.
Learn about World War II.
Learn about Colonial America.
Learn about the great missionaries of the past.
Learn about gardening and cooking.
Learn about home improvement.
Learn about golfing, decorating, or lawn care.
Learn about science.
Learn about math.
Learn about the ministry.
Learn about leadership.
Learn about philosophy.
Learn about forms of government.
Learn about medicine.
Learn about finances.
Learn about the law.
Learn about strategy.
Learn about self-discipline.
Learn about geography.
Learn how to travel.

Learn about Washington, Lincoln, and Reagan.
Learn about the Civil War.
Learn about literature, art, and poetry.
Learn about parenting.
Learn about psychology.
Learn better communication skills.
Learn how to sell.
Learn how to exercise.
Learn how to write.
Learn about love.
Learn about the grief of losing a loved one.
Learn how to play an instrument.
Learn how to forgive.
Learn how to improve your marriage.

Knowledge increases your potential to succeed at starting a business or following a career path you've always wanted. Somebody, somewhere, who is no smarter than you, has done it. If they can, there's a good chance that you can.

Knowledge can help you live outside your insecurities. Memoirs and fiction often allow the reader to hear the thoughts of the characters as they navigate through life. Rather than living as a constant prisoner of the procession of your own thoughts and feelings, you can begin to visualize yourself as a character in your own story. You're the author of your novel. Make the main character do what is best.
Knowledge can empower you to have the emotional depth to

The Solution: Reading Books

be a better lover or friend. Love stories, narratives of loss, and accounts of great passion and sacrifice enrich the sentiments. Some of the classics, in one novel, convey a quality of feeling that some will never experience in a lifetime.

Knowledge can give you a broader perspective. Most of us have tunnel vision, seeing the world from a single point of view, namely our own. Like Aristotle's geocentric view of the universe, it's easy to see things as though they revolve around you. Others are considered only as they relate to you. Racism, hate, and selfishness seem inevitable when you realize that the earth's population consists of billions of people that imagine the world with themselves at the center. Reading can help you see the world through someone else's eyes. Imagine a world where everyone sees their personal existence in its proper place—a soul created by God to love the Creator and their fellow man as much as they love themselves; not better than the pauper and no less valued than any king.

Knowledge will raise the bar on personal expectations. The biographies of George Mueller, Marcus Littrell, George Washington, Simon Kenton, and Horatio Nelson make me feel like an absolute loser, but they also make me want to be better. London, Dickens, L'Amour, and Dostoevsky's fictional characters often convey their author's idealism in a way that inspires me to strive for honor, dignity, and manliness.

Knowledge in any field can make the mind sharper in other,

often unrelated, fields. No matter what I'm reading, the more I read, the more mentally efficient I feel in every aspect of my life. C.S. Lewis, in "Mere Christianity," postulated that a Christian life would make an individual the best version of himself. Similarly, I would suggest that reading can help you to become a much better rendition of you. The hope is not that we will become some cookie-cutter intellectual, but that we will be sharpened and strengthened in our own unique gifting.

Reading can make you humble

I'll never forget the first time I visited a planetarium. Seeing the earth as a speck of dust in the vast expanse of space made me feel small. When I finished the last line of *Anna Karenina*, I felt like a tiny intellectual pebble overshadowed by the Everest-like intellect and emotional depth of Tolstoy. Where did Churchill find the time to save the world, govern the British Empire, and write vast historical volumes? While reading George Mueller's autobiography, I told myself that the reason he was able to build orphanages without ever asking for donations was that he was so much older than me. I was humbled to discover that he was younger than me when he did most of his work. How could Grant direct a battle on horseback while the whistle of musket balls mingled with the shrieks of dying men and yet not so much as flinch? How was Simon Kenton able to survive the brutality of the American frontier? How did La Valette, as an old man, inspire a small group of greatly

31

outnumbered Knights to hold the tiny island of Malta against the mighty Ottoman Empire? I don't have answers to these questions, only impressions; I feel small, insignificant, and humbled. When I say the word humble, I don't mean spiritual humility. Of course, humility is a virtue, and I hope to be as humble as possible. What I am talking about is the feeling of being entirely overawed by people who work harder than me, discipline themselves more, practice consistently, pray often, and live better than me. It is humbling.

There's an old story of a family acquaintance who was a fantastic basketball player. He was dominant in his college years. In one of his first experiences at the NBA level, he walked onto a court where some players were shooting around. According to the story, the confident newcomer jumped and grabbed the rim and asked, "Whose team am I on?" One of the players who had been around for a while jumped up and grabbed the top of the backboard and said, "Not mine." The older I get, the more that story sounds like fiction. However, it illustrates a point perfectly. We can become overconfident when we spend all our time with equals or inferiors, but mingling with those greater than ourselves and contemplating their high ideas inspire us to keep our heads down and strive to be better.

Tenaciously pushing forward is only useful if you're moving in the correct direction. Stubbornly refusing to compromise your ideas is great, if your ideas are right. The world has enough bulldogs; what it needs is somebody that knows something. Yes! Stand up for your faith but make sure you know what you believe. Consider a matter from its various facets. The world isn't monochromatic.

I cannot say that I always enjoy the feeling of inferiority as I read about great men and women around the world and throughout history. However, the greatest thing I have learned over the last decade is how very little I know. Honest and realistic self-awareness is solid ground upon which to start trying to improve.

Reading can make you quiet

The love child of ignorance and arrogance is excessive talking. I have a theory; IQ can be measured by how much unsolicited talking one does in a group. Less talking is an indication of more intelligence.

Why does ignorance induce speaking? Here are some possibilities:

- The self-confidence produced by ignorance assumes intellectual superiority.
- From a me-centric perspective, everyone in a group has gathered around to hear my opinions.
- Ignorance misses social cues such as wandering eyes, heavy sighs, nervous glances, and not-so-

subtle excuses to exit the group.

- A lack of exposure to information makes any recent exposure new and exciting. That new information is assumed to be just as exciting for everyone else.
- Ignorance assumes authority on any subject if it was seen on the news, heard at work, or remembered from junior high gym class.

It would be easy to assume that becoming an expert on a particular topic would make a person talk more. However, that doesn't seem to be the case. Why would that be? Perhaps:

- Learning increases sensitivity to social cues.
- Social situations are understood to not be lecturing opportunities.
- Learners learn by listening.
- Experts are aware that giving justice to any topic would take more time than a social encounter might comfortably provide.
- While ignorance produces arrogance that needs to lecture, knowledge produces quiet that is at peace forbearing.

Maybe, while reading the preceding paragraphs, you've been asking yourself why I, the author, think I can judge between the ignorant and the intelligent. Here's my qualification for being able to speak on this topic: I spent many years of my life being ignorant, and I've been around people who are intelligent. I've been in thousands of conversations where the desire to talk overcame me as powerfully as steam from a pressure cooker. Barely able to comprehend what they were saying, I would watch the mouth of the person speaking, waiting on that magical moment when they would stop talking, and I could interject my comments. My four favorite words in social situations were, "I," "me," "my," and "mine."

Then there were those conversations with people I knew to be intelligent. I waited, in vain, for them to impart to me from their vast wealth of knowledge. That's what I would've done if I were them. However, to my surprise, their part of the conversation was dominated by questions—"What business are you in?" "How is your family doing?" "Now what part of Indiana are you from?"

For a significant part of my life, I thought that questions like those above were proof of just how exciting I was. I can remember conversation after conversation, prattling on about myself. I have just enough pride that I'd like to go and find some of those people, and when they ask me a question about myself, I'd like to respond with one sentence that answers their question, ask them a question in turn, and then listen as long as they want to talk.

Below is my idea of a man who puts the power of knowledge to work. The setting is a committee meeting. The task of the

35

group is to provide clean water solutions for an impoverished village.

> First, this man has spent years reading and thinking about affordable, clean water solutions. That's why he's **qualified** to be on the committee.
>
> Second, he has come to the meeting with some well-thought-out theories.
>
> Third, he sits **quietly** during the meeting introduction, opening discussions, and while several ideas are put forth.
>
> Fourth, he jots down pros and cons of the various proposals and asks questions.
>
> Fifth, if the ideas presented are superior to his own, he works to support their development.
>
> Sixth, if no good proposals emerge, as a clear leader, he pays proper respect to the ideas put forward and then makes his presentation.
>
> Seventh, he invites sound critique of his ideas. Eighth, if his proposal doesn't stand up to a thorough examination, he humbly supports the

group as they seek other solutions.

Maybe I should be writing a book entitled *How to Make People Think You are Intelligent in Social and Business Situations."* Probably not. First, that title is too long. Second, you can paint a barn, but it will still be full of manure.

Knowledge will make you qualified, humble, and quiet. It will increase your ability to influence people and impact situations. Maybe you're saying, "I'm all for knowledge, but I still hate reading." In the next chapter, I'll address alternate sources of learning. Spoiler alert: I don't think there is a shortcut to real knowledge. Reading takes time. However, the resulting knowledge is worth the effort.

CHAPTER FOUR
There Are No Substitutes

Our bodies need vitamins and minerals to live. Any kind of food is going to have some level of nutrients in it, but the nutrients-to-calories ratio means that some foods are way better for you than others.

According to the *My Fitness Pal* app, four ounces (one hundred calories) of grilled chicken has twenty-two grams of protein, four percent of your daily iron, and two percent of your calcium and vitamin C. According to that same app, a five hundred eighty calorie serving of chocolate pie has five grams of protein and no vitamin D, calcium, iron, potassium, vitamin A, or vitamin C. That is almost six times the calories with significantly fewer nutrients. There are some good things in a slice of chocolate pie. You might even be able to survive by eating only chocolate pie, but it is definitely not an efficient way to stay healthy.

There are many ways to learn, but they are not all created equal. Visual media, the internet, periodicals, and traditional learning formats may be the most popular ways of learning. In this chapter, I want to explain why I think they may also be the most inefficient.

Visual Media (Movies, TV, YouTube)

There I was, at seven years old, sporting my footy-pajamas, and holding my Tupperware bowl filled with Cheerios covered in a half cup of sugar. All I wanted to do was watch the Roadrunner drop an anvil on Wiley Coyote's head. And then… "This is your brain. This is your brain on drugs—a sugar induced high. Any questions?" … suddenly the way I looked at eggs was forever changed. That experience helped me make up my mind that I didn't want my brain to get fried by narcotics.

Drugs allow a person to have a powerful experience without doing anything to earn it. When a person comes down from the high and returns to typical real life, their old normal now feels like misery. The next time they take drugs, they have to take more to get the same high. So much beauty and value is lost "chasing the dragon."

That 1980's sugar-induced high which I turned into an anti-drug commercial is how I think of the effects of visual media on the brain. Television, movies, and YouTube videos are like opiates. You can crawl out of bed and plop down on the couch, smelling like your favorite sweat pants that you just found in a gym bag from last month. Pick up the TV remote, and the world is at your fingertips. You can view the world from the top of Mount Everest. You can feel the terror of being chased around a house by a chainsaw-wielding murderer.

You can feel the thrill of being a part of a love scene with an A-list actor or a tantalizing supermodel. Yesterday's games are being replayed for your reviewing pleasure. What's more, the scenes are reduced to just the highlights. You don't even have to watch the boring pitching series, timeouts, foul balls, or any of the other mundane plays. You can be romantically motivated, horrified, brought to tears, laughing, screaming, and cheering, all within a few minutes and with absolutely no effort. You don't have to climb the mountain, learn the sport, or even take a shower. Your brain doesn't even have to form the images. It's all served up to your synapses without you lifting a single grey cell to make it happen.

You may be asking, "What is wrong with that?" Glad you asked: two things are wrong.

First, during the thousands of hours we spend looking at media, over a lifetime, our brains turn to mush. "How's that?" you ask. Just imagine a weightlifter trying to maintain his strength by watching people pump iron. The analogy isn't exactly equivalent, but it's close. Your brain goes on autopilot while you watch media.

Secondly, when you've been in a love scene in your rancid sweat pants with a supermodel, your regular old wife just doesn't seem that great. When you can sit on the couch and enjoy almost every emotion known to man without doing anything, real life starts feeling a bit mundane. Going to work is hard, and the benefits are slow in coming. Keeping your job is hard. Getting along with your boss is hard. Mowing your lawn, taking out your trash, taking a bath, cleaning your car, being a mom or a dad, being a good spouse, going to church, putting on your outside clothes before you go to Walmart, and a thousand other things are hard work, and the emotional payoff of these mundane tasks just can't live up to visual media.

A third reason visual media is an inefficient way of learning is that there is a tremendous amount of bias you have to navigate through to get to anything educational or even entertaining. Here is a fun little exercise for you: find out how many individuals own the majority of media outlets (i.e., Turner Broadcasting, Yahoo!, YouTube, etc.) I think the answer will surprise you. No wonder I can't find a sweet and straightforward, family-friendly, animated feature for my nine-year-old daughter and me to watch together.

Please consider these actual quotes from me while trying to watch a cartoon with my daughter:

"Ahh, aren't the bunnies cute?"

"Audrey, bunnies are NOT the result of millions of years of natural selection by random chance."

"I know the bunnies are cute dear, but mob justice isn't

okay even for bunnies. The bunnies have to follow the rule of procreation."

"Dearest, just because bunnies have been doing what they do for a long time doesn't automatically mean their traditions are malicious lies passed down from their bunny-forefathers as a means of mind-control."

"No, honey. The mating habits of bunnies are not closely related to that of cave dwellers in the Paleolithic period."

Click

"Do you want to go outside and play?"

Radical social ideas are subtly injected through modern media. It goes something like this: The main character is a detective. He is single. He is good looking. He has a modern high-rise apartment. He is smart and just. He always has the right words. He always sticks up for the underdog. In this particular episode, he is investigating the mysterious deaths of several terminally ill patients. Are these crimes being committed by a serial killer? Is it greedy relatives that can't wait for life insurance payouts? Maybe it's a psychotic nurse. No. In the end, it turns out to be a kind, beautiful, and benevolent doctor who is helping these patients escape from their misery. She knows that the unjust laws declare her to be a murderer. However, she is willing to risk it all for the good of the suffering people. When the handsome detective discovers what's going on, he is moved with great affection for the heroic doctor. However, in the end, he has to uphold the cruel and unjust laws that forbid doctors from having mercy.

The subtlety is ingenious. We are led by the nose right down the path to euthanasia. If producers just came right out and said exactly what they meant, we would reject it outright. Nobody would buy it if a four hundred pound, greasy, pitted-skin TV executive came right out and said, "Murder the old geezers so society doesn't have to support them. Whack the sick, and we can split the money. And, by the way, kill the babies or this planet is going to get so crowded that somebody will have to live in Nebraska!" I don't expect them to be that honest anytime soon. Until that time comes, I'm going to find my information somewhere else. Furthermore, I'm going to try to make sure that my kids are getting their information from a better source.

I've personally witnessed ideologies overshooting subtlety and landing right in the middle of absurdity. I was thrilled to attend my first presidential inauguration with my son and my father. Your political affiliation is immaterial for this story, for this was first-hand experience for me. There were so many people it was overwhelming. Public transit systems were jammed. Streets were flooded. Every security checkpoint was clogged with thousands of people. Everywhere you looked there were Trump lovers, MAGA hats, suits and ties, and smiling faces. The most violent thing we witnessed all day was when Chuck Schumer's face showed up on the big screen TV in front of the section where we stood. The crowd got downright ornery. The three of us stood in one spot for seven hours, barely able to move due to the crowded space, half starved, and mostly frozen. Later in the day, we tried to get to the street where the parade was going by. However, thousands of people were being turned away because they just couldn't fit. We had heard so much on the news about protesters that we were looking for them all day long. We counted seventeen scraggly, dirty, school-skipping teenagers cussing and carrying vulgar signs. Seventeen! I was absolutely astonished by how the major news networks covered the inauguration. According to them, the day was overshadowed by massive protests and a pitifully small crowd. The contrast in being there and hearing the reports sounded like two different places. I couldn't believe it. Anyone that was there knows that those news reports were untrue. From this experience I developed an axiom: Just because it's in the news doesn't make it true. A better maxim might be equally significant: Anything in the news is probably questionable.

Visual media is too often biased at best: it will diminish the joy of everyday life. You have to sort through the mountains of garbage to get a little bit of worthwhile information. It's not worth it. What is your favorite steakhouse? Imagine going to that steakhouse with Ted Turner. You order your favorite cut of meat. Thirty minutes later a friendly waitress hurriedly places a hot plate, steak still sizzling, in front of you. That beautiful, perfectly marbled and succulent steak is just waiting for you to indulge your craving. However, instead of letting you eat the steak yourself, Ted reaches over and takes it from you. You watch as he chomps it up and swallows it. You're a little taken aback when he burps with delight. However, you're entirely unprepared for what comes next. He vomits the meat back out onto the plate. And then like he's making something special, with fork and knife, he forms the half-digested meat into a shape that roughly resembles a steak. Then he pushes the plate across the table to you. Is that how you like your steak? I don't want my information that way either. I'll eat my own steak, Ted. Thank you very much.

The Internet/Google

The Internet can make studying much more convenient than it has ever been. You no longer need a dictionary, a set of encyclopedias, expensive commentaries, a dozen different translations of the Bible, or a library of the classics. All of that is available online and for free. I use all of these resources quite frequently.

However, I have found so much of the information online to be unreliable. First of all, bias is pervasive. While much online information sources are not outright lies, the inclination of their authors makes the information dubious. Let me give you an example. I'm going to describe the same man in two completely different ways.

> Description one: He's old, fat, and hairy. He wears bright colored pants. He's usually a recluse, but every now and then he comes out in the middle of the night.

> Description two: He is an elderly gentleman, portly and jovial. He's a man of great talents and vast resources, but he devotes all his time and wealth on philanthropy. He's honest, principled, and just. He lives with Elves in the North Pole.

> Both descriptions are technically accurate (or false depending on your view of Santa). However, it is evident that the prejudice of the first author makes the information nearly worthless.

After reading Tolstoy's *Anna Karenina*, I looked up the novel's character list on an online site that claims to accurately summarize books. I was surprised to discover that Anna Karenina was actually some kind of champion for women's rights in a world hostile to women. Really? That's what Tolstoy wrote? Wrong! If you have read the book, you know beyond a shadow of a doubt that Anna is a self-serving adulteress who abandons her family for pride and lust. In the end, she is completely destitute, and there is no hope of restitution. Tolstoy's summary of life is to obey God's law and love people—that summary is mine. Anybody who reads the online summary would think Tolstoy was a champion of the modern women's liberation movement. I would encourage you to read the book for yourself. In doing so you can judge Tolstoy for yourself, and you can also determine the validity of the online summary of the book.

There are some excellent questions to ask before trusting a resource. First, who wrote it? Can you believe the author? Do your homework. Second, a fitting axiom for determining trustworthiness is, "Follow the money." Who paid for this site? Who paid for the research? Who has a vested interest? For sites like Wikipedia it's impossible to answer any of those questions. Crowd-sourced sites are also not impervious to inaccuracy and bias. Look up President Donald Trump on Wikipedia and ask yourself if the information is fair or even close to complete.

Furthermore, regarding the President, any Google search about President Trump will return almost exclusively negative information. I am not trying to defend the President. However, to suggest that nearly all of the conversation regarding the President is negative is inaccurate. Almost half of all the people in this country voted for him, and there are millions of passionate supporters. How is it that the positive side of the conversation is nearly nonexistent in Google results? We all need to be reminded that Google, Yahoo, Vimeo, YouTube, Facebook, and Twitter are all private businesses owned by people. These people have politics and passions. We need to keep that in mind every time we use our computers.

Often, online resources lack references. As a side note, the inclusion of references doesn't guarantee that the information will be unbiased. A quick look at the list of references may reveal prejudice at the very heart of the work. Many internet-based sources lack references altogether. I've watched online videos that claimed to make difficult subjects, like theoretical science, simple. Sure, it was simple. It took one side of the research, converted theories to absolutes, presented partial information as conclusive evidence and used the medium of animation with a decent narrator and *voil*à. The only problem with the program is that it's highly speculative, unproven, and there isn't a single bit of research cited. But, how many people have watched that video and walked away thinking that they know the truth about the subject?

One last note about online media. It need not be true. I'm no website designer, but I know enough about *Wordpress* that I could create a website this afternoon. That website could make a thousand claims and not one of them be right. I could say ninety-nine things that are true and state one lie. I could make up a religion, create a false history, or fabricate a chemistry experiment. Excepting libel or slander, there are no laws about telling the truth. I wonder what percentage of the people that came across my site could decipher the truth from the lies. I wonder if the ones who are inclined to trust my site would do any research to determine if it is true or not.

Podcasts, Newspapers, Magazines

Often, when discussing the subject of reading, people tell me that they listen to a lot of podcasts. Although I think listening to podcasts is better than nothing, I don't think it can be called reading's equal. I would lump listening to podcasts and reading newspapers and magazines into one category. This type of reading/listening isn't as efficient as reading a book. Imagine that you are hungry for a steak. You drive down the road to a local farm where you see some cows. You buy a cow and take it to your house where you kill and butcher it. You find a cut of meat that looks good, take it into the kitchen, and fry it up. Yummy! When you listen to a podcast or read the newspaper, you are "buying a cow." The information itself is unrefined. Additionally, the format of the information is unrefined. The author of a book may spend months or years refining his own information and literary mechanics until he finally produces a work with which he's happy. The producer of a podcast, or magazine, or newspaper article may discover and publish their information in a matter of hours. It is "meat on the hoof." It then becomes the consumer's job to refine the work into usable information. It is my opinion that you are much better off skipping the pasture in preference of something a bit more refined.

I could consume "two thousand calories" of YouTube videos, newspapers, podcasts, and online research and not gain one ounce of reliable material. It is as likely as not that much of what I consumed would be misinformation. There is a better way to learn. In the next chapter, we will begin to discuss practical methods for becoming enlightened.

CHAPTER FIVE

Reading Books: The Best Way To Learn

There are three optimal ways to learn: travel, hands-on experience, and reading. In this chapter, we will ask six questions about each one of these learning methods:

> *What are the distinct advantages?*
> *How much will it cost?*
> *How long will it take?*
> *Is it safe?*
> *Is it possible?*
> *Is it convenient?*

1) Travel

Advantages of travel

Some things can only be understood by being on location: tasting the food; smelling the air; feeling culture as you are immersed in it. I'm going to take several paragraphs to share some of the highlights of my personal travel experiences. In a book about reading, I may be taking a bit too much time talking about my excursions. Feel free to skip forward in this chapter to the heading, "The Cost of Travel." However, if you're interested in my little travelog, here you go.

Lost in Prague

I wanted to experience the beautiful and historical city of Prague but not like a tourist. From the window of our hotel, I could see what looked like an ancient castle perched on top of the hill in the center of the city. I took a good look at my map, folded it up, and put it in my pocket. I walked briskly, looking up only occasionally. I just glanced at street signs, as if I knew my way around. I should've known that I would never be able to find my way back without taking some notes. There were street names like "Olšanské hřbitovy," "Kralovské Vinohrady" and "Rajská zahrada." Try to say one of those three times quickly. Between narrow streets, I would occasionally catch a glimpse of the castle, and I was eventually able to find it. I climbed one of the tall towers and took dozens of pictures of the city from that vantage point. One of those photographs is the only art I have hung in my home.

As I left the castle, I knew that I needed to go toward the river. However, I was unaware that the river looped back so that I could cross the river traveling North or East. I needed to go East, but that didn't happen. I had walked about 4 miles when I started seeing green meadows and knew that I needed some directions. I had been told that everyone in Prague speaks English, which I discovered isn't exactly right. From my experience, no one in Prague speaks English. I swallowed my pride and took my map from my pocket. The problem was, I had no idea where I was. I found a little old lady and showed her on the map where my hotel was. I made hand gestures to indicate that I needed to know where I was on the map. She looked at me inquisitively and then pointed about 2 feet above my map. I pointed this way and then that and shrugged, "Which direction do I go?" With her crooked little finger, she indicated the right direction, and a couple of hours later, I stumbled into the lobby of my hotel, a newly minted Prague-enthusiast.

Drunk on Cherries

On our way to Skopje, Macedonia, the birthplace of Mother Teresa, my travel companion and I stopped so that we could buy snacks and gifts to give away to impoverished children. He bought several boxes of chocolate covered cherries. At some point in the trip, he began eating the cherries and loved them. Later that night he still had several boxes of them. My friend was an adventurer, but he was usually a pretty serious guy. That's why I was surprised by how much talking and laughing he was doing during the car ride back into Greece. He would eat a couple of cherries and then talk and laugh and carry on. I had never seen him like that before. I became suspicious about the candy. I said, "Let me see that box." Sure enough, the ingredients, in order, were: cherries, alcohol, chocolate, et cetera. I think that was the first and only time my friend, who was a conservative minister, had ever been tipsy. He practiced absolute abstinence toward alcohol. I laughed until I cried. He didn't laugh anymore that night or the next day. I still feel a little bit bad that we gave all that candy to the gypsy children. I hope they were okay.

The Front of the Line

While in Rome—with the same friend who gave liquor bombs to gypsy kids—we decided, last minute, to visit the Sistine Chapel. Little did we know that we needed to hire a tour guide or wait in line for several hours. The string of people waiting to get in was over a mile long. We pondered the situation for a moment until my friend said, "Let's go to the front of the line." At first, I adamantly refused, but then I reluctantly acquiesced. We walked passed thousands of people and walked straight up to the guards that were letting people in, one at a time. My travel companion said that we didn't have time to wait and that we needed to be let in immediately. At first the the guards absolutely refused. However, he persisted. "Please, just let us in." After a few humiliating moments, the guards gave in to his demands. I could not believe it, and I was irritated. I don't know if I was upset because we looked like pushy Americans or if it was because I knew that I would never have had the guts to do that myself. For him, he really wanted to see the Sistine Chapel, and he was also paying me back for having such a laugh over the cherries at his expense. I think I could write a whole chapter about fighting in Austria, getting sick in Rome and finding a bathroom with not a moment to spare, joining the children of a grade school in Armenia for their field day, eating gyros in the shadows of the Parthenon, and visiting the monasteries of Meteora.

My son and I traveled to Spain, Tunisia, and Malta. On that trip, we discovered Antoni Gaudí's Sagrada Família in Barcelona. We learned that purchasing a second rate ticket on the train in Tunisia means you'll be jammed in a cattle-type car with standing room only, and so, of course, the doors will be open. Late that night, searching for food, we wandered the narrow streets of old Tunis lined with elderly men smoking hookah pipes. We ended up on top of an old building in an open-air restaurant with a view of the whole city. As I drank the sweetest cappuccino imaginable, the Adhan drifted across the air from a distant mosque. In the next few moments, what must've been a dozen more calls to prayer joined in dissonant harmony from all across the city.

Special Guests

The Tunisian taxi driver found us roaming around the city and offered us his services. I did my best to get rid of him, having had some bad experiences with taxis. Before the day was over, we would leave expensive camera equipment in his car while we visited tourist sites, and we even gave him a large amount of cash to deliver to a street vendor to whom we owed money. It was this self-appointed tour guide that introduced us to the

Roman amphitheater where their national festival was taking place that week. My son and I determined that we would return later that night for the concert. During the taxi ride back to the amphitheater that evening, my son fell asleep. That in itself was amazing because our taxi driver was traveling more than one hundred kilometers an hour, weaving in and out of traffic. Somehow the bumper of our taxi got caught on another car and was ripped loose. The driver pulled to the side of the busy highway, jumped out and used a piece of rope to tie the bumper back on. He climbed back into the car, and once again we merged with traffic. My son never stirred.

We arrived quite a bit early and waited for security to begin allowing people in. We found a place to sit in a large open area that led up to the amphitheater stage. As we were waiting, police began to arrive and secure the area. At first there were just a few, but within a few minutes, a large group of officers had organized. They blocked off all the entryways and escorted everyone out of the area; everyone except Matthew and me. We began to get uncomfortable, knowing that we weren't supposed to be there and that we would eventually have to get up and walk out of the area to join the large and growing group that was assembling outside the gates. During this time, police officers would approach and greet us. One officer asked Matthew if his tie was straight. I was tense because I knew we were not supposed to be in this area, and I wondered why they hadn't kicked us out. Also, within weeks of our arrival, the country had experienced brutal terrorist attacks, and I knew that they were on high alert. Finally, I told my son that we had to leave. We got up and awkwardly walked across the open area and out of the gate. I could feel the eyes of every officer on us. We joined the group of several thousand people waiting to go through the security checkpoint. About this time an agent from the gate approached Matthew and me and said, "You will be at the front of the line." He ushered us past several thousand people that were waiting and took us all the way to the front of the line. We were the first people into the amphitheater that night. To this day I have no idea why.

If a picture is worth a thousand words, seeing a site first hand is worth ten thousand pictures. I'll never forget visiting the Grand Mosque in Muscat, Oman. Its main chandelier measures forty-five feet and weighs eight and a half tons. It consists of six hundred thousand crystals and has 24-carat gold plating. The prayer carpet in the men's prayer area contains one million seven hundred thousand knots and weighs twenty-one tons. This hand-woven carpet measures two hundred thirty feet by two hundred feet and covers forty-six thousand square feet. However, I think the humility of the imam was more impressive than the physical structure itself.

The cost of travel

Travel is one of the two most expensive ways to learn. While college, on average, is more costly, tourism is a close second.

For a young, single person traveling with a companion (I don't recommend anyone traveling the world alone.), it's not cost-prohibitive. For every person in your life that you don't want to leave behind, the price increases. If you are flying, that increase is dramatic. For a married father of three, the price tag is out of reach for most.

Time to travel

It takes months to plan a good trip. Schedules have to be coordinated. You have to shop for reasonable flights; find hotels, Airbnb's, or hostels; and plan ground travel. Of course, traveling itself takes time.

Is it safe?

Most travel is reasonably safe, especially if you have a traveling companion. However, there are some places you desire to learn about to which you wouldn't want to travel because of a lack of safety. I had the opportunity to go to Turkey with my son. After doing a little research, I realized that the place we were visiting was less than ten miles from the Syrian border. That region was experiencing a lot of terrorist activity. I did not feel like it was safe at the time. I opted to take my son to Honduras. Little did I know that the Honduran murder rate was twice as high as the second highest murder rate in the world. To get to the house where we were staying, we had to navigate a series of roadblocks with armed guards. The house itself had an automatic steel gate, broken glass lined the upper story of the house, as well as electrical fencing. During that trip, the man we were with lost his parking ticket in a shopping center garage. While he searched frantically for it, I asked, "What's the big deal? How much could it cost?" Our driver said, "You don't understand. Without a parking ticket, we don't get out." He didn't tell us what he was going to do. He slowly approached the exit where a guard stood holding a shotgun. As the armed man approached us, our driver slammed the accelerator and sped away. My son and I crawled into the floorboards of the vehicle anticipating gunshots.

Needless to say, not everywhere you desire to travel is safe. I was threatened with violence by a homeless man in D.C. He had told me to leave the park where I was filming. Past the edge of the viewfinder of my camera, I saw him sneaking up on my right-hand side. I'll never forget him yelling, "You're a lucky man!" as I ran away. I was almost arrested in D.C. for filming on a tripod in front of the Supreme Court building without a permit. Apparently, that's illegal.

Is it possible?

It is not possible to travel to every place that you may want to learn about. Unless you're an astronaut, you won't be going to space. Unless you're a diver, you won't be experiencing the depths of the ocean. Unless you're an experienced climber, El

Cap is probably beyond your reach. There are many places you're just not allowed to visit. You can't visit the Oval Office without an invitation. You can't explore a nuclear missile silo or the palace of whichever Kim Jong is in power. Without a time machine, you can't travel to the signing of the Declaration of Independence, the surrender of the Japanese fleet, or the discovery of King Tut's tomb. Furthermore, even with a Time Machine, you can't visit theoretical musings about the future.

Is it convenient?

It can be convenient to take your kids to Mount Vernon or on vacation to some beautiful sunny place. However, there are some places to which it's just not practical to take a family. Even if I had the money, the time, and I felt like it was reasonably safe, I don't think my ten-year-old is suited for hours of sitting, sipping a cappuccino, and contemplating the greater meaning of life from some European street café.

Although it's expensive, time consuming, inconvenient, and maybe even dangerous, some things cannot be understood until you are there. So, there are a few places in the world that you'll probably have to visit. If you're anything like me, you'll cherish the memories the rest of your life.

2) Experience

Advantages of hands-on experience

If you want to know about strawberry ice cream, eat some. You'll learn more from one bite than from a ten thousand page book about it. If you want to know what it feels like to free-fall, then try skydiving. If you're going to see sharks in the wild, dive. If you want to know what it feels like to get married… well, you get the picture.

You can learn to drive a stick shift in five minutes. I don't know if you could ever learn that skill from a book. There are thousands of other things that can best be learned by hands-on experience.

The cost of hands-on experience

Learning to drive your friend's stick-shift will probably be free. Many hands-on experiences are. However, killing big game in Africa is prohibitively expensive for most.

Time for hands-on experience

Learning to bake chocolate chip cookies doesn't take a lot of time, but becoming a concert pianist might take you a lifetime.

Is it safe?

Here's where reading and hands-on experience really diverge. Although some lessons are perfectly safe, many others aren't. For example, bow hunting for grizzlies, building your own still, engaging in mixed martial arts, free climbing, skateboarding, drag racing, police work, firefighting, and active military service all include elements of danger.

Is it possible?

There are many accessible experiences that you should try. If your options are 1) sitting on the couch and watching someone else do something exciting, or 2) going out and trying it yourself, choose to do it yourself nine times out of ten. But some things, for a thousand practical reasons, just aren't possible.

Is it convenient?
If your friend is a mechanic and wants you to help him restore a classic car, you'd be crazy not to do it. However, if you just want to learn about restoring classic cars and you don't have access to any equipment, rather than investing your life savings in something you were just curious about, it might be time to look to the third way of learning—reading.

3) Reading

Advantages of reading

Authors from nearly every country and language, who are experts in their fields, have written about almost every subject you can imagine. They have spent years researching, practicing, traveling, thinking, and performing in their various areas. They record in books all of the experiences that they deem valuable. Their knowledge and expertise is available to you in the form of books.

Even if you traveled to Paris and spent a month studying Da Vinci at the Louvre, and even if you could smell the local boulangerie and taste the Soupe à l'oignon, what do you really know about Paris? Can you really know about it without understanding the balance of power in Europe, the World Wars, Napoleon, and de Gaulle? Can you take its pulse in a few days without feeling the passion of Proust or Hugo? Can you understand France without descending into the Bastille or hearing the unmistakable *thwump* of the guillotine? But men and women have studied the art for years, have grown up smelling the bread, lived through World Wars, and marched next to DeGaulle, and they have written about it.

The cost of reading

Reading books is, by far, the cheapest way to learn. Nearly every town in America has a library where you can borrow books for free. Goodwill and other thrift and consignment stores often have a great selection of extremely cheap books. Usually, there are books in garage sales, and people will practically give them away. Public domain books are available online in digital format for free. Several companies offer audiobooks at very reasonable rates. Unless you are required to have a degree, rather than spending thousands of dollars on college classes, borrow the books from the library for free. If cost were the only factor, reading books would win the contest of the best method of learning, hands down.

Time and convenience of reading

People often say they don't have time to read. I beg to differ. Past and present presidents of the United States, CEOs, inventors, entrepreneurs, ministers, and stay-at-home moms find time every day to read. You can read in the morning or last thing at night. You can read during a lunch break, waiting for a doctor appointment, waiting in line at the grocery, or at a restaurant. You can have books in your bedroom, bathroom, car, your desk at work, and on the living room end table. Reading a legitimate book a few minutes a day would probably put you in an elite category of informed people on planet Earth.

Is it safe?

I don't recommend reading while walking down the street, while driving a car, or while your spouse is talking, unless it is an audiobook. However, I don't recommend listening to audiobooks while your spouse is speaking.

Is it possible?

While reading a book, everything is possible. You can descend to the depths of the ocean to research a shipwreck or go twenty leagues beneath the sea to fight giant sea monsters. You can go to the Moon, Mars, or fight aliens on Venus. You can join the inner circle of every president that has ever held office. You can accompany an inventor through the thousands of failed attempts to develop some new technology. You can go into the lab without a key card. You can become knowledgeable of law without passing the bar. You can soar with a test pilot or perform with a soprano. You can trudge through the jungles of Vietnam or plant a flag on Everest. Nothing is beyond the reach of a reader.

The best way to learn

Reading is the best way to learn. Reading offers the advantage of the inner thoughts, passions, and expertise of many of the most exceptional people who have ever lived. You can read for free. Reading is the most convenient and time-friendly way to learn. It is safe, and anything is possible when you read.

CHAPTER SIX
You Can Love Reading

I was about five years old the first time my mother put beets on my plate. They were the color of cherries, moist, and sliced like cranberry sauce. Those beets looked good enough to bypass my usual new food routine. Typically, it took me a while to warm up to unfamiliar items, but those beets had some serious plate appeal. I stuck a whole slice in my mouth and began to chew, and just as quickly, I almost threw up. It was a while before I had that kind of blind faith in a vegetable again. A single bad experience with a food item can taint your opinion for a lifetime. However, I don't hate vegetables; I just hate beets.

I spent over thirty years of my life saying that I hated to read. As it turns out, I don't hate to read, I just hated what I was reading. This life-changing revelation began in a Borders Bookstore across the river from Cincinnati in Newport, Kentucky. My father was doing a book signing for his then-latest novel, *Bloodroot*. While we were there, a book caught my attention. The book was *To Hell and Back* by Audie Murphy. It was a cheap paperback, and I was curious, so I bought it. The following day I reluctantly began to read my new purchase. I couldn't put it down. A couple of days later I was stunned to realize that I had read the book cover to cover, and I absolutely loved it. That moment could not have been more revelatory even with a choir of angels singing in the background. I realized that I didn't hate to read; I only hated what I was reading.

In the thirty years that lead up to that moment, I had read a handful of books. So, that night I went to my bookshelves and pulled out every book that I had read start to finish. There were less than ten. I wanted to see if the books that I had read had anything in common. They did. Almost everything I had read was a memoir, and most of them were military memoirs. I was on to something.

Within a few days, I was back at the bookstore looking for another memoir chronicling someone's battle experiences. The book I purchased was Stephen Ambrose's *Citizen Soldiers*. I began reading it, and to this day I still haven't finished it. That was a fail. So I tried again and hit pay dirt. I read *Alexander of Macedon* by Harold Lamb. Then I read George Bush's *Decision Points*. By then I was off to the races, and I never turned back.

The key was that I only read books I wanted to read. If I didn't crave it, I didn't read it. I also made a deal with myself that if I started a book that I ended up not liking, I would not finish the book. I skipped the "Don't you know there are people all over the world that don't have any books?" routine. I never cleaned my plate unless I loved it. The first book I didn't finish was *Dutch*, by Edmond Morris. That sad excuse for a biography was a "beet" to my pallet. I skipped books I didn't enjoy and gave into my literary cravings. The result was a burgeoning appetite to read. And so my journey began.

If you're a book hater, I would suggest that you skip the Brussels sprouts and go straight for the dessert table. What are you interested in? Find one small book with positive reviews on a subject of interest. If you love it, read it. If you don't love it, return it or put it on the shelf and try again. Give it a try. I am convinced that most people don't really hate reading. They just hate *what* they are reading.

CHAPTER SEVEN
How To Find A Good Book

I propose to you that the reason most people don't love reading is that they have never had a wonderful experience with it or that they have had a bad experience. It's like a person that is standing beside a turquoise blue pool of water on a sweltering day, and they don't want to jump in. Either they've never swum before, or they have had some kind of traumatizing water experience. Okay, maybe there's some weirdo out there who learned to swim as a child, has lots of positive memories about it, but just doesn't want to get wet. Those people are the exceptions.

What has happened? Maybe you read too slowly, or you've never really read a book you liked. Or perhaps you went to high school, and the teacher forced you to read *The Scarlet Letter* or *Wuthering Heights*. Maybe you still think history is a giant list of names, dates, and places. Honestly, I don't know what teachers are thinking. What's the best way for a person to learn? Reading. Let's force feed raw unsalted volumes down students' throats until they swear they'll never read again. If the only thing kids learned at school was how to read and a love for reading, they would become learners for life.

How To Find A Good Book

If you're not in love with reading, but you want to be, the most critical step is finding a book that you enjoy. Don't start with a commitment to reading that is an act of self-discipline for you, like saving money or going on a diet. Allow your reading appetite to develop naturally. Don't pick a book that you "should" read. Just because you're an engineer doesn't mean you need to whet your appetite by reading *Newton's Principia*. Don't start with raw broccoli. Maybe you should eat a cupcake instead. Begin by picking a book by an author or about a person that you really like. Do you love George W. Bush? His autobiography, *Decision Points*, might be of interest to you. Hate George W. Bush? Maybe you should read *Shrub* by Molly Ivins and Lou Dubose.

Read something about a subject that piques your curiosity. Rather than high math, maybe you should read a travel journal by Krakauer or a memoir that takes you places you never dreamed of going. Love baseball? Try reading *The Glory of Their Times* by Lawrence S. Ritter. Do you want to laugh? *Dad is Fat* by Jim Gaffigan is a great choice. Pick up a book that sounds interesting or exciting.

I have a rule for myself. If I start reading a book and discover that I don't like it, I don't read it. Even if I spent fifty dollars on a book, if I don't like it, I don't read it. I do not force myself to read anything. Why? Because I now love to read, and I don't want to taint that passion with bad books. Sure, I have wasted some money on books that don't even deserve to be on my bookshelf. However, I still love to read, and that makes it worth the cost.

Where do you start? Amazon offers dozens of categories and millions of choices. How do you reach into that haystack and pull out the one book that you will find appetizing? You can narrow the field and increase your chances of finding a good book by following the recommendations of others. It is pretty simple. Do a web search for, "Book recommendations by Bill Gates" or "Elon Musk" or "Steve Jobs" or anyone else you might trust.

Often, non-fiction, autobiographies, memoirs, and biographies will list books that the author or person who is the subject of the book recommends. Follow those leads. I was a fan of George W. Bush's presidency. After reading his autobiography, I tried to read every book that he recommended. From those books, I found new leads, and as a result, I had some of the most favorable reading experiences of my lifetime.

Below I have listed partial, suggested reading lists from sixteen different people according to various sources. I would recommend that you pick one book from one person's reading list. If you love it, and there are leads, follow them. If you don't love it, or there are no leads, go back and try again. Even if it takes you weeks or months and several books before you find one that you like, the effort will be worth it. Please note that there are several books on this list that I have not read.

How To Find A Good Book

Neither am I endorsing the books on this list. I will make my own book recommendations in chapter fourteen.

- **Ernest Shackleton**
  The Brothers Karamazov—Fyodor Dostoyevsky
  Thou Fool—JJ Bell
  Voyage of the Vega—A. E. (Adolf Erik Nordenskieöld
  The Morals of Marcus Ordeyne—William J. Locke

- **Bruce Lee**
  The Amazing Results of Positive Thinking—Norman Vincent Peale
  The Athlete In The Making—Jesse Feiring Williams, M.D. and Eugene White Nixon, M.A.
  The Complete Amateur Boxer—Bohun Lynch
  Kill Or Get Killed—Col. Rex Applegate
  Think and Grow Rich—Napoleon Hill

- **Steve Jobs**
  1984—George Orwell
  Atlas Shrugged—Ayn Rand
  Inside the Tornado—Geoffrey A. Moore
  Moby Dick—Herman Melville
  The Innovator's Dilemma—Clayton Christensen

- **Ivanka Trump**
  Meditations—Marcus Aurelius

Leaders Eat Last—Simon Sinek
Shoe Dog—Phil Knight

- **Elon Musk**
  Structures—J.E. Gordon
  Benjamin Franklin: An American Life—Walter Isaacson
  Einstein: His Life and Universe—Walter Isaacson
  Superintelligence—Nick Bostrom
  Zero to One—Peter Thiel and Blake Masters

- **Jeff Bezos**
  Built to Last—Jim Collins and Jerry I. Porras
  The Innovator's Dilemma—Clayton Christensen
  Sam Walton: Made in America—Sam Walton
  Lean Thinking—James Womanck and Daniel Jones
  Memos from the Chairman—Alan Greenberg

- **Meghan Markle**
  The Motivation Manifesto—Brendan Burchard
  The Inner Gym: A 30-Day Workout for Strengthening Happiness—Light Watkins
  When Breath Becomes Air—Paul Kalanithi
  The Tao of Pooh—Benjamin Hoff
  Who Moved My Cheese?—Spencer Johnson

- **George S. Patton**

  R. E. Lee: A Biography—Douglas S. Freeman
  Genghis Khan, Alexander of Macedon, and other biographies by Harold Lamb
  Memoirs of Ulysses S. Grant
  The works of Rudyard Kipling
  The Prince"—Niccolo Machiavelli

- **Louis L'Amour**

  Treasure Island—Robert Louis Stevenson
  Ben-Hur—Lew Wallace
  Don Quixote—Miguel de Cervantes
  My Life on the Plains—George Custer
  Lives—Plutarch

- **Henry David Thoreau**

  Works of Aristotle
  Works of Cicero
  Natural History—Pliny
  Ralph Waldo Emerson's essays
  A Peep at Polynesian Life—Herman Melville
  Voyages—Jacques Cartier

- **Abraham Lincoln**

  Aesop's Fables
  William Blackstone Commentaries
  A Practical Treatise on Pleading—Joseph Chitty
  George Balcombe—Nathaniel B. Tucker

Pride and Prejudice—Jane Austin

• **Theodore Roosevelt**

Life of Alexander—Benjamin Ide Wheeler
Abraham Lincoln—John Hay and John Nicolay
Bacon's essays
Call of the Wild—Jack London
Virginian—Owen Whister

• **Bill Gates**

Factfulness—Hans Rosling
How Not to Be Wrong—Jordan Ellenberg
Tap Dancing to Work: Warren Buffett on Practically Everything, 1966-2012—Carol Loomis
Stress Test: Reflections on Financial Crises—Tim Geithner
The Bully Pulpit: Theodore Roosevelt, William Howard Taft, and the Golden Age of Journalism—Doris Kearns Goodwin

• **George W. Bush**

Team of Rivals—Doris Kearns Goodwin
Next—Michael Crichton
Executive Power—Vince Flynn
The Coldest Winter: America and the Korean War—David Halberstam
American Lion: Andrew Jackson in the White House—Jon Meacham

- **Pope Francis**
  Lord of the World—Robert Hugh Benson
  Notes from Underground—Fyodor Dostoevsky
  The Spiritual Exercises—St. Ignatius of Loyola
  The Lord—Romano Guardini
  The Return of the Prodigal Son—Henri J. M. Nouwen

- **Martin Luther King Jr.**
  Civil Disobedience—Henry David Thoreau
  The Social Contract—Jean-Jacques Rousseau
  Republic—Plato
  The City of God—Augustine
  Nicomachean Ethics—Aristotle

CHAPTER EIGHT
Finding Your Long-term Motivation

In this chapter, I want to share two disappointing probabilities and encourage you to push past them. First, most people don't care what or how much you read. Second, you may not notice any immediate benefits from reading. Experiencing these disillusioning realities is normal. Don't give up. Reading yields rewards beyond the illusions. Reading changes you similarly to the maxim, "You are what you eat."

When you start reading, you're going to want to talk about it. You'll be excited about the books and just the fact that you are reading. At first, friends and family will be supportive, maybe even impressed. "How many books did you read? Wow! That's amazing!" However, in time, it's likely that you'll notice a steady decline in interest in the fact that you are a reader. Unfortunately, you might even find people disinterested in the exciting things you're reading about. It's possible that even readers won't care. They might just be waiting for you to stop talking about your book so they can share theirs. Do you know why? Because nobody in their life cares about what they're reading either. They're hoping you'll be the listener that you want them to be. Bummer.

Non-readers who start reading are a novelty like a guy going on a diet. In his book, *Finding Ultra*, Rich Roll tells the story of his journey from an overweight attorney to an extreme athlete. On the eve of his fortieth birthday, he struggled to walk up the stairs. Three years later he would be named one of the "25 Fittest Men in the World," by *Men's Fitness* magazine. I'm sure people were all ears on the first day of his diet. "You're not eating that?" I'd bet that his friends and family wanted to know all the details of his first few runs. Eventually, seeing super-fit Rich Roll just reminded people how fat they were. Rich must have had a motivation that went beyond obtaining the approval of friends and family.

I still remember the joy I got from subtly slipping details about my infant reading life into conversations. It was like bringing a newborn to a party. That same kid six weeks later just isn't all that interesting anymore. You know, maybe my child wasn't that amazing to begin with. Perhaps he was just another average kid like the other six billion that were newborns at one point. There are probably a few genuine baby-lovers; the rest of the people never really cared. They were just being nice. Bless their hearts. If you're reading to please people, that satisfaction will last a couple of weeks. What then?

The second hard reality I had to face about reading is that I didn't experience any obvious immediate benefits. This may be due to the kinds of books I read. I suppose that I could have read books about topics I'm facing right now.

My daughter has been a little bored lately. I could read about entertaining teen females. I need a new car. I could read a book about negotiation. That kind of reading sounds a little like the Whack-A-Mole game at Chuck-E-Cheese. That isn't how I choose books. Often, while reading, I'm asking myself, "What am I ever going to do with this information?" I like to read long history books for no obvious reason. It's like somebody pulls up with a dump truck load of pea gravel. "Where do you want me to put this?" the driver asks. "Uh…. Put it here in my brain. I'll sort it out later." Am I just wasting time? What is the point?

You are what you eat, but the results take time. If you want to be strong, you don't walk into a gym thinking, "Two hours from now I'll be a power-lifter." You don't eat leafy greens expecting to be lean and mean in the morning. Reading, to me, is like mental, emotional, and spiritual nutrition. If you read the right stuff, in time, it will begin to shape you. I'm not looking for a quick reference; I'm focused on the long-goal, which is becoming the person I want to be. I'm reading this today in preparation for something. I'm not sure what, but I want to be ready when I get there.

In 1941, while the world was at war, Dwight D. Eisenhower was the Chief of Staff for Lieutenant General Walter Kruger's Third Army in San Antonio, TX. Eisenhower had not been able to "get to the scene of action" in WWI. Now, it seemed that WWII would pass him by as well. Colonel Walter Bedell

Finding Your Long-term Motivation

Smith phoned from Washington. "Is that you, Ike?" It was a summons to come to D.C. for a meeting with George C. Marshall, Chief of Staff for the Army. Eisenhower assumed that he was being brought to Washington because of his knowledge of the Philippines, where he had previously been stationed. This was only the fourth time Eisenhower had seen Marshall and the first time they had spent more than two minutes in conversation. Marshall spent twenty minutes informing Eisenhower of the situation in the Pacific and then abruptly asked, "What should be our general line of action?" Eisenhower asked Marshall to give him a few hours. He was assigned a desk, and he began to formulate an answer. However, his deliberations didn't start then and there. Eisenhower had spent years studying worldwide military matters. He was prepared. Eisenhower gave Marshall his advice and Marshall responded, "I agree with you." He then said, "Do your best to save them." That one brief meeting set in motion a course of events that, six months later, would catapult Eisenhower to the position of Commanding General, European Theater of Operations. It pays to be prepared.

I'm not reading so that I can tell people I'm reading. I'm not even reading to have something to talk about. I'm not reading to serve a short-term need. I'm preparing. I believe that I'm on my way to an important rendezvous. I am convinced that somewhere and sometime, opportunity will come to give me my chance. I intend to be prepared for that meeting. Of course, I'm not talking about suspended life, doing nothing, just waiting. I'm talking about struggling, sacrificing, improving, saving, practicing, failing, and working hard where I am, all the while preparing. I'm reading in between every one of the elements of life, believing that Pasteur had it right, "Fortune favors the prepared mind."

CHAPTER NINE
Expanding Your Appetite

In this chapter, I want to deal with two parts of the same issue: developing reading taste. First, if you're not an avid reader, don't let your lack of literary appetite discourage you. Even if you aren't reading at all now, you can develop into a reader with a highly diverse palate. Second, if you do read, it's essential that you develop your reading taste buds so that you are getting the value out of the time you're putting in. Periodically, I run into an avid reader that never goes outside of a narrow field of interest. That's not good, especially if that limited interest is mystery, romance, sci-fi, or the like. If you're lifting weights, your body doesn't care if you're lifting iron or watermelons. However, that doesn't hold true for reading. If you don't, at some point, read something with real substance, the activity will not yield the benefits that it otherwise could. If romance is what you have to read to get started, read romance, but don't stall out in the process. Keep moving forward.

When I was two months old, my diet consisted of milk that was 98.6°, give or take a degree. During that happy phase of my life, I developed what would become a lifelong love affair with eating. Thank you, Mother, for not starting me out with meatloaf. Today, if you mention Chinese, Mexican, Greek, homestyle, or just about any other cuisine (maybe excepting German), I get giddy. Although I have been known to dabble in pasties without much coaxing. Developing this skill was simple. First I had milk, then pureed fruits and veggies, then Mac and Cheese, then nuggets and fries, then pizza, steak, and eventually, with reluctance, sushi. Everything else fits somewhere in between. I don't force myself to eat. I don't feel like a hero when I eat five thousand calories in a day. It's as natural as breathing and a lot more fun.

The process I just described is precisely how my reading palate has developed. First, it was military memoirs: lots and lots of them. Eventually, I developed a taste for military history, then general history, and so on.

Don't be concerned if you aren't interested in anything outside of one or two areas for the first few months of your reading journey. Don't force it. Find books that you love to read. If you keep reading, I guarantee that you will begin to develop a higher capacity to enjoy an ever-widening range of subjects.

Start small and then expand the circle. If you start with fiction, you could add historical fictional. Work your way into a biography. Once you discover an era, nation, family, or individual of intrigue, you will find it even easier to expand from there.

Start with a novel that takes place in Paris. Maybe you'll become curious about the city and its history. What made Paris what it is? For that matter, France? Then perhaps you'll be ready for *A Tale of Two Cities*. Or you might follow the path of Napoleon to the battle at Maloyaroslavets. Maybe you'll be interested in *War and Peace*, or perhaps you'll want to skip forward to Waterloo. How did the Iron Duke forge an alliance that defeated Napoleon? The leads can go on forever. With every step of expansion, your knowledge will increase as well as your craving for more.

You can expand your reading appetite by following leads, even if you start with a comic book.

Calvin and Hobbes (kids' comic book) → *Looking for Calvin and Hobbes: The Unconventional Story of Bill Watterson and his Revolutionary Comic Strip* (Biography) → Plato (political material that influenced the cartoonist according to *The Complete Calvin and Hobbes*) → Plato's *Republic* → *Greek Philosophy: Thales to Aristotle.*

Maybe that seems a little extreme, but it's just how literary taste develops. It's hard to know where this exciting process is going to lead.

I'm clearly still in this process. There are dozens of broad fields that I haven't even touched yet. My reading diversity is as follows:

Expanding Your Appetite

History - 21%
Biography - 24%
Classic Literature - 3%
The Sciences - 14%
Business - 4%
Religion - 18%
Sports - 1%
General Fiction - 15%

I want to continue expanding my reading experience. In addition to the kinds of books that I'm addicted to reading, over the next two to three years, I want to read a minimum of five books in each of the following categories:

Literature (drama, poetry, and prose)
Performing arts (dance, music, and theater)
Visual arts (drawing, painting, filmmaking, architecture, ceramics, sculpting, and photography)
General Science
Botany
Zoology
Biology/Anatomy
Life Origins
Chemistry
Math
Astronomy
Psychology/Psychiatry
Sociology
Language

Sports
Fiction

I talked to a voracious reader-friend of mine the other day. For him, anything outside of non-fiction, business-related material is worthless. When I first started, I thought fiction was a complete waste of my time. However, in addition to Louis L'Amour (previously the only fiction I would read), I have discovered some authors who have set my mind ablaze. Tolstoy's grasp of the world is awe-inspiring. As I finished the last pages of *Anna Karenina*, I felt so small. I wandered into the bedroom where my wife was working, and I sat on the bed with tears in my eyes. "I thought I was smart," I said. "Now I feel like an intellectual pebble nestled insignificantly in the shadow of Tolstoy's Everest-like intellect."

Wells, MacLean, Clancy, Flynn, and Crichton, while maybe not changing my life, have added something of real value to it.

Read whatever seems appetizing to you. Follow leads to related fields of interest. Don't stall out in the process. By doing so, you'll develop your reading hunger and strengthen your mind along the way.

CHAPTER TEN
Audiobook Workaround

At this moment I'm sitting in a Starbucks with my dad's latest novel, *God of Our Fathers,* laying on the table in front of me. It's the tenth book he's written and the most recent novel that I'm afraid I'll fail to read. My father is a great writer and my hero and mentor. On the cover of this book, I claimed to be a bibliophile. I have a stack of books that I've wanted and attempted to read for years. What is my problem? The problem is, at one hundred sixty words per minute, reading a physical book is slow and painful. That's why I don't do it.

Yep, you read that correctly. A guy that is writing a book about reading does not read physical books. At least not very often. The problem isn't just speed but also comprehension. Apparently, the slower you read, the lower your comprehension. That makes reading a real blast. I'm flying through a page like a glacier races through the millennia, get to the end of the page and say, "Huh?" I'd rather dust blinds than sit and read a book. Sitting down to do nothing but look at black characters in neat rows on paper is my intellectual equivalent of eating beets by the bucket.

Three-hundred-words-per-minute readers make me mad.

Audiobook Workaround

What really irks me is people who can digest a book in one sitting yet choose not to. That is like the 6′ 8″ guy in high school who doesn't play basketball. What a waste of height! There's all these 5′ 8″ wannabes running around with their tongues hanging out saying, "Pick me, coach! Pick me!" I'm still certain that somebody switched my body at birth because this 5′ 8½″ cannot be what God intended. I wanted to be good so bad.

One of my fantasies is sitting smugly in a coffee shop with a book, reading away the hours. Instead, I'm sitting here with my phone, earbuds, and writing instead of reading. And it's painful for me to read even what I write. Sad.

I figured out that I love what is in books, but it is hard to get that stuff off the pages and into my head. I'm like a toothless lion staring longingly at the hind-quarters of an antelope: drooling and crying. In the words of that comic scholar, Brian Regan, "How do I get that goodness in me?"

Maybe you thought you were hopeless because you read slow and have low comprehension. There are dozens of books claiming to increase your reading speed. It might be worth it to you to check some of those out. Although, that's like a doctor prescribing walking to a guy who's struggling to walk. "If you'd lose some weight, your knees wouldn't hurt when you walk. If you'd walk, you might lose some weight."

"I hate to read."

"There's a good book about that. You should read it."

Wow! I digress. What I understand is if you increase your reading speed you'll also remember more of what you read. Low intelligence is probably not the problem. In reality, because your brain isn't getting enough stimuli, it wanders off in search of something more engaging.

A second option might be to hire someone to read to you. They could stand right between the palm-waving eunuchs. If reading a physical book or hiring an equerry doesn't sound practical or desirable, you might try listening to books.

Listening is the ultimate solution to my reading dilemma. In contrast to my loathing of reading words on pages, with all my heart, I absolutely love to listen to books. I consider it to be fun. It's a thrill. I'd rather listen to a book than do just about anything. Before I discovered audiobooks, reading came in just above a prostate exam on my list of things I enjoy. Today, listening to books takes third place behind spiritual devotion and family time.

Full disclosure: I still don't look cool in coffee shops listening to audiobooks while I sip *horchata* frappuccinos. I listen to books while doing a wide range of other things: mowing the lawn, vacuuming, driving, showering, waiting on whatever, running, riding a bike, painting, drawing, eating, waking up, going to sleep, and yes, dusting blinds. I love to read on the go. When I'm stuck in one place, I listen while playing some kind of inane game, like solitaire, on my phone. I can feel my heart and nerves calm as I settle into a chore or into bed while I listen to a good book. It has been life-transforming.

I have learned and grown more in the last eight years than I had in the previous thirty-five. Reading, through listening to books, was the opening salvo to that revolution.

There are several audiobook services, including Audible, Scribd, and Overdrive. I have used Audible almost exclusively. I have the app on my phone, and it works nearly flawlessly. All the books that I own are available to me at any time. I can take notes, set a timer, and change the speed of the reading. The subscription is reasonable, and the service is impeccable. I can return any book that I have purchased, any time, for a full refund. Audible is a no-brainer for me. It is worth every penny.

I'm not trying to push you to audiobooks. I'm suggesting that you don't abandon your reading journey because you've encountered a roadblock or two. It's worth it to you to figure out what will work for you. In my opinion, there is no alternative to reading that even comes close to its benefits.

If you do decide to give audiobooks a try, I would also

recommend wireless headphones. Oh, what a difference they will make, especially in the shower!

One final word on finding the method that works best for you: if you are that smug nerd lounging with a book at the local cafe, I don't like you. It's not right. It should have been me. But if you squander the reading gift that God has given you, I hope, nay, even pray that you are hit with a late case of adult-onset ADHD, ADD, or restless leg syndrome. Be afraid. Be very afraid.

CHAPTER ELEVEN
Plot Your Course And Track Your Progress

To me, of all the various kinds of exercise, road cycling is the least sadistic. Don't get me wrong, it's still torture, but it's more like the Chinese-water variety than keelhauling. I'd rather be drawn and quartered than to jog around the block. Cycling is similar to fun. It was one of my favorite activities in childhood, and I can burn calories doing it. However, when I'm thirty miles from home on a hot day, and my Gatorade is gone, waterboarding actually doesn't sound that bad. "Oh? Water? Sounds refreshing!" I try to ride fifteen to twenty miles two or three times a week with some bigger rides scattered throughout the year. One thing I never do is ride fifteen feet without turning on the Map My Ride app. It's kind of like, If I didn't record the ride, it didn't happen. If my phone is dead, I'm not riding. Why? There is something powerful about having a record of what's been done and having a plan for how to improve.

Maybe, for some, being tarred and feathered sounds more appealing than being staked to a book for any amount of time. Contrasting that aversion, for the reader, there's great satisfaction in looking back and down from a conquered summit and seeing the scaled renderings of past challenges.

Plot Your Course And Track Your Progress

Each pitch is a trophy, and the steeper, the better.

Plotting a course and tracking progress enriches a life of reading. Make a plan, set goals, and keep a written record.

A mentor often said to me over the years, "writing down your thoughts gives them the power of legitimacy." I think he was right. Unorganized ideas are like feral cats: they're always there—mating, meowing, eating, marking their territory, and vanquishing the bird population—but they never really accomplish anything positive. You have to round up those cats into a herd. Then you can go to town and hire some "catboys" and have yourself a little cat-drive. Don't let your cats rule you; take those little suckers to market. That's precisely what I think my old mentor was thinking. What I mean to say is write stuff down.

I suggest a digital version of your "to read" list, goals, and "books read" list. It's best if you can access it anytime and anywhere. For example: when you're on vacation and you discover a huge used bookstore, or when you're trying to think of a book you read two years ago. If you're reading physical books, keep a slip of paper in the book with notes of things that seem significant. Additionally, when you finish the book, you could take a picture of your notes that you keep in your digital records. On audio apps, use the note-taking feature to keep track of your thoughts.

- Create and write down your goals.
- Keep a running list of books you want to read.
- See a book that looks interesting but not ready to buy? Write it down.
- If someone makes a book recommendation, write it down.
- Write it down when an author mentions another book.
- Is there a particular author or subject you'd like to read? Write that down.
- Don't rely on your memory.

How many books do you want to read this year? If you read two last year, maybe you could read ten if you worked at it. Maybe twenty-five. You could be aggressive and shoot for a book a week. My ongoing, annual, minimum-reading goal is one book for each year of my life. I'm forty-six at this writing, so I need to read a book every eight and a half days.

Getting ahead of my goals is rewarding. It makes me feel like an overachiever. When I fall behind, I'm challenged to get in gear. Or, sometimes I just read a couple tiny books. That's fun, too. And, it doesn't matter. Nobody cares about what I'm reading or not reading anyway. This isn't for them.

Keep a running list of books you've read.

The other morning I woke up crammed up against my wife

and lying on my unplugged phone. I had drifted into dreams the night before while reading to my wife my list of "books read" this year. Apparently, I bored myself to sleep. I go back and read my list several times a month. Sometimes I go back several years to reminisce about the reading experiences I've had.

Keep a list for your own reference. Periodically, I'll remember some snippet of a story or concept but can't remember where I got it. I'll go back over my list until I find that book or books I think it might have come from. Then I pull out that book and go through my written notes, whether physical or digital. More often than not, I'll find what I'm looking for. It pays to write it down.

Write down book title and author(s). You can also keep track of the number of pages and/or the genre. Number your list for easy reference. I want to know, at a glance, how far along with my annual goal I am. Keep a running total from year to year and update your total books read at the end of each year. As the stacks start stretching towards the ceiling, there's a feeling that I've done what I should. I can sleep better at night knowing that I'm making a real effort to be the man I'm supposed to be.

CHAPTER TWELVE
Read Something Old

For the love of perspective, read something that isn't on the New York Times current best-seller list. Read some books that are old. We don't have to be star-struck with the past, but we don't need to get all of our perspectives from the razor's edge of the present perspective of the past. There are a million miles of knowledge under our feet. Read something old, something that's out of print. "Hindsight is 20/20" is right in that we can see what's happened better than we can see what hasn't. However, on a long, straight road, sometimes it's significant to look in the rearview mirror. The farther you get from something, the harder it is to recognize or understand it. Reading something old connects the distant past to the relevant present. It's significant to do this without the injection of someone's current view of the past. Current views are often faulty interpretations of the past.

New books are being written all the time about subjects like the fall of Rome, the US Civil War, and the first lunar landing. But I just don't think it's necessarily true that the journalist with his still drying XYZ University diploma has a clearer perspective than Tacitus, Grant, or Armstrong. You know there were actually people there the day that Rome was built, and some of them wrote about it.

I'm sitting here in a nice little coffee shop called, Quills, in Indianapolis, Indiana. The coffee is good, but the patrons come across to me as a bit, well, unreal. All the guys are wearing tight-fitting jeans and lumberjack-looking shirts. I don't know how all these loggers are keeping their boots so clean. They also have Civil War era beards and manicured fingernails. Every woman in the room is wearing spandex. Did I stumble into a cyclist club or a drama club? What a mismatch! If all these lumberjacks hook up with all these bikers, we're gonna have a slew of ax-wielding Lance Armstrongs. Of course this could make one more curious about the Tour de France.

Granted, I may just be feeling my age, sitting here in my slacks and button down, but come on! There's something else going on here other than my failure to keep pace with the trends. These people are all getting their cues from each other. They may be reading, but I think they're reading blogs. I'm surrounded by hoards of Johnny-come-latelies infused with massive amounts of confidence induced by shortsightedness.

The past still speaks for itself, without modern interpretation. Maybe these iPhones haven't changed the world that much. Perhaps all this tech is just the latest smoke signal shouting from an adjacent hilltop. Who cares how we say it? It's what we're saying that matters. Maybe someone has been here before. Maybe they shared their insights on a crackling rotary phone or clicked it out on a telegraph, or perhaps they etched it into stone, but "their" words have value today. Maybe they lived in times like this long before us. Perhaps we should heed their warnings. Moses shouts from the wrong side of the Jordan, and Solzhenitsyn calls to us from a gulag. Anne Frank, in silent turmoil, set the quill to paper. To read her words touches the emotions, and a tear flows down one's cheek as freely as a stream cascades over hills and into the valleys. The years have not diminished the poignancy of these writers, but the past will keep its secrets if we only see from the razor's edge present. Relive the past from the eyes of the authors, not the interpretation of the commentator or teacher. Read the past in the exact words penned by the author, not the conflicted ideas of the critic.

All that's new is not revolutionary, and not all revolutions are helpful. Sometimes they're just bloodbaths that cleanse people from hope and freedom. How can we know what causes to embrace and which to dismiss? How can we avoid the tragedies of the past and stand on shoulders straining to see hope that brims on new horizons? Listen to the echoes of the past. Our fathers wait with great suspense for us to open their letters and let them speak again.

CHAPTER THIRTEEN
Connect The Dots

When I was a kid, I drew connect-the-dot pictures. In preschool, the art consisted of twenty or thirty dots that turned out to be the outline of a puppy or a rabbit. As I got a little older, there were more dots and more complex pictures. More dots equals greater detail. Fewer dots means a much simpler rendering. No dots, no image.

Every book I read is like another dot on my worldview. Each new disclosure creates increased complexity and reveals details yet unknown to me. There are angles I had never considered and realities I didn't know existed. There are great people who have lived and died, learned, loved, conquered, suffered, succeeded, and left behind roadmaps of their journeys. Today I remain ignorant to all but a few of them. Here a dot, there a dot, and vast swaths of territory yet shrouded in fog. Extraordinary lives remain inert on bookshelves around the world. Their old lessons learned are again mysterious to a new generation. Tens of thousands of books have been carved out of the granite of real life; each page is painstakingly etched with humanity. Fortunes have been gained and lost. Love has been found and squandered. Passions, like rivers, have flowed across the landscapes of time, snaking trails of history worth knowing. Existence is so hard. Contestants free-solo over life's sheer facets, plotting courses that we can follow. They belay ahead of us, but their timesaving, life-saving help is hidden on dusty shelves between cloth and cardboard. Generations of non-readers, again, brave the treacherous cliffs of life with no rope. If each generation struggles away at discovering the old paths all over again, how can we ever move forward?

It's thrilling to discover an important historical figure, period, political system, or debate unknown to me. It's also embarrassing to realize that our modern world is literally built right on top of ruins about which I've been completely ignorant. The Roman statesman, Marcus Tullius Cicero, circa 46 B.C., is quoted as saying, "Not to know what happened before you were born is to be a child forever. For what is the time of a man, except it be interwoven with that memory of ancient things of a superior age?"

I grew up unaware that my maternal grandpa was part of the decoy army on D-Day, that he was at the Bulge, or that his were some of the first boots to touch soil east of the Rhine. There is a book, *First Across the Rhine,* that chronicles nearly every day of his journey, struggling, building, and fighting in Europe. How can I know who I am without knowing where I came from or who has gone before me? Now I know. Another dot has been added. Who was Grandpa's commander? To which army was his engineer combat battalion attached? Who was the general of that army? Dot, dot, dot. Am I an expert on

WWII now? Far from it. A dozen books deep, the most explicit image I have is of my glaring ignorance. Oh, what a beautiful revelation that jars me into silence! I'm no authority. I'm a novice following the trail left by my forebearers. The glorious revelation of my ignorance shuts my mouth and piques my curiosity. I don't know, but I could if I will read.

It thrills me when I'm reading a general historical work and discover along the journey some man or idea that I know a little something about. I just ran into a dot that I found and noted somewhere along the line. The view from the new perspective reveals something even more. This is learning, and it is addictive. There are other genres just waiting to be known. History, languages, political science, art, botany, philosophy, and many more, like eager children, wriggle on shelves screaming, "Pick me!" They will not keep their secrets. Open their covers and they'll tell you everything they know as they dutifully add their dot to your canvas. You will profit from their disclosures for a lifetime.

George Bernard Shaw said, "He who can, does; he who cannot, teaches." Perhaps there are some who would say, "He who can, does; he who cannot, reads." I'm not suggesting that you check out of life and read instead. If you have the option to love or read about love, love. If you have the opportunity to paint, or read about painting, first, learn how to paint, then paint. Or, paint in the basement and leave your work there for your kids to find when you really do check out.

Walk, ride, love, give, work, build, and explore. I might say, "When you can, do; in between, read." Leave the TV off, put the computer back in its bag, stop producing, stop talking, turn down the tunes, and read. Let the words rush over you. Let them puddle in phrases and ideas until rivulets gather in torrents of inspiration. When they recede, they'll reveal a rock or boulder, and maybe gold. Even if it's just a pebble, it's another dot, and the world is clearer.

I started this book with nine reasons why I hated to read. Below is a list of fifteen reasons why I now love to read. If you experience just two or three of these benefits, reading would be well worth the effort.

1. It makes me better at my work.
2. It helps me live outside my insecurities.
3. It increases my emotional depth.
4. It inspires me to want to do great things.
5. It helps me think about things that matter.
6. It opens up new areas of interest for me.
7. It promotes humility by reminding me that I'm a pretty average guy.
8. It makes me talk less.
9. It is great entertainment.
10. It is the cheapest, safest, and quickest way to learn.
11. It removes the boundaries of time and space.
12. It puts me inside the minds of great people.
13. It prepares me for once-in-a-lifetime opportunities.

14. It teaches me the lessons of the past.
15. It gives me a broader perspective of the world.

If there were only two things I could give my kids, a love for reading would be one of them. Tonight, between bites of her sirloin, my ten-year-old, Audrey, shared some interesting details from "What Was the Wild West?" by Janet B. Pascal. Mission accomplished! At seven o'clock this morning, I received a text from a young friend of our family with a quip from Glenn Livingston's, "Never Binge Again." Young people giving reading the nod gives me hope for the next generation. Being a part of that process gives me a feeling akin to helping my firstborn take his first steps. Though I may never meet you, through this book, I hope I have helped you discover the gift of reading. In time, reading will be more valuable to you than gold, more meaningful, less toxic, equally as addictive, but without the long-term complications.

I hope that when you put this book down, you will begin your search for a great read. That will make my efforts in writing this book quite fulfilling. The final chapter is my list of recommendations. Happy reading!

CHAPTER FOURTEEN
My Book Recommendations

After years of struggling to read a book, I finally realized reading was possible for me. I simply had to find books I enjoyed and realize I couldn't literally read them; rather, I had to listen to them on some electronic device. Once I conquered these two dilemmas, I disciplined myself to branch out into various subjects and authors. Now I love reading. I hope I've helped you on your journey. To conclude, here's a sample of books I've read. Perhaps you, too, can enjoy some of these.

Books that teach

The History of WWII Vol. I-VI—**Winston Churchill**
This is the exhaustive history of WWII. It is educational, inspiring, massive, and terrifying if history does repeat itself. This six-volume masterpiece is daunting. When you're about to pass up this work because of its sheer size, just remember that one man wrote it, and he did so without a computer. The weaknesses of great people, the courage of Great Britain's populace, the pettiness of some, the magnanimity of others, and the "Triumph and Tragedy" of war on a worldwide scale are all on display in this *pièce de résistance.*
Catastrophe 1914—**Max Hastings**

My Book Recommendations

My great-grandfather, Harry Weatherholtz, and his brother struggled in the morass of WWI against hunger, cold, wounds, and the enemy. Nevertheless, I knew nothing about "The Great War" until I read *Catastrophe 1914*. Through the first chapters, Hastings bulldozes through mountains of details. I struggled at first to find my pace, but when I read the closing line, I felt like I was saying goodbye to a dear friend. I will most certainly make this journey again.

Memoirs of William T. Sherman—**William T. Sherman**

He failed in business; he was frequently morose; he probably suffered a nervous breakdown. By contemporaries and adversaries, he was mercilessly ridiculed, but he ruthlessly pursued southern armies in a campaign that ended on the Eastern Seaboard of the US and ended the South's hopes for independence. In this grueling, sad, but ultimately triumphant saga, I find hope for a life of intermittent successes and failure. Apparently, an unbroken succession of wins isn't a prerequisite for purpose. In the end, presidential glory came knocking. He never would answer.

Decision Points—**George W. Bush**

If your attitude about George Bush's presidency is in harmony with CNN's, and you like it that way, don't read this book. There's so much to know about Bush's eight years in office that you won't learn from liberal media. Was he a bumbling warmonger? What happens if you remove George Bush from the scene from 2003 to 2011? Read McCarten's *Darkest Hour* and ask yourself what would have happened in Europe in the 1940s without Winston Churchill. What if Churchill had been Prime Minister in 1936 when Hitler moved into the Rhineland? Would Churchill have ordered preemptive strikes on an overtly aggressive burgeoning German war machine in time to downgrade a world war into a police action? It's a sad reality for George Bush's presidential legacy that we'll never know what tragedy might have happened without it.

Personal Memoirs of Ulysses S. Grant Vol. I-II—Ulysses S. Grant

General Grant's memoir is straightforward, self-effacing, and powerful. It is part history, part leadership coaching—before leadership was a thing—and part Mark Twain-style storytelling. If you think Lee was a genius and Grant was a butcher, this book will give you another point of view. Grant seeks to set the Civil War record straight.

War as I Saw it— George S. Patton

If anyone "saw" WWII, it was George Patton. He had a front-row seat, bought with blood, sweat, and tears, in the splash zone. He was the William Tecumseh Sherman of the twentieth century and no less committed to victory. If you're a man, you need to read this book to find out how to be one. If you're a woman, you need to read this book to get an idea of what a man is supposed to look like. Through the millennia, one in a billion babies is born without the rational capacity to be afraid, doubt themselves, or give up. Patton was that baby. I wouldn't be surprised if someone told me Patton came out of the womb in an army helmet and wielding an ivory-handled revolver. Additionally, he was an avid reader. Surprisingly, I don't recall one curse word from the whole book.

New England's Memorial—**Nathaniel Morton**

There's traditional American history with turkeys and top hats and then there's history revision. How does anyone know anything about what happened on those shores of Massachusetts? Of course, we must study the source material. Nathaniel Morton's *New England's Memorial* is some of the best source material available. As a Separatist settler in the Plymouth Colony, he lived the harrowing birth of a colony that would become a new nation. Why take anybody's retelling of the story when you can read an eyewitness's account for free on Google Books or purchase your own copy for less than $15 on Amazon?

Democracy in America—**Alexis de Tocqueville**

"Virginia was home to the first English colony. Immigrants arrived there in 1607. Europe at the time was still singularly preoccupied with the idea that gold and silver mines constitute the wealth of nations: a disastrous idea that did more to impoverish the European nations that embraced it, and destroyed more men in America than war and iniquitous laws combined. It was, therefore, gold-seekers who were sent to Virginia, men without resources of discipline whose restless, turbulent spirit caused trouble for the colony in its early days and rendered its progress uncertain. No sooner was the colony created than slavery was introduced. This capital fact was to exert an immense influence on the character, laws, and entire future of the South.

"It was in the English colonies of the North, better known as the New England states, that the two or three principal ideas which today form the basis of the social theory of the United States were first combined...The civilization of New England was like a bonfire on a hilltop which, having spread its warmth to its immediate vicinity, tinges even the distant horizon with its glow...The people who immigrated to New England brought with them admirable elements of order and morality...what distinguished them most of all from other colonizers was the very purpose of their enterprise...They tore themselves away from the pleasures of home in obedience to a purely intellectual need. They braved the inevitable miseries of exile because they wished to ensure the victory of an idea... the Puritans sought a land so barbarous and so neglected that they might still be allowed to live there as they wished and pray to God in liberty."

These quotes are found in the second chapter of the first part of Volume I. These are not the ramblings of some alt-right operative. They are the honest reflections of a Frenchman in the mid-1830s. This book should be required reading for every American.

My Book Recommendations

Rush Revere—Rush Limbaugh

The five books in Limbaugh's *Rush Revere* series, covering the story of America's founding fathers, is in a format suitable for children, teens, and me. My ten-year-old daughter couldn't put them down. I totally could have; I just chose not to. They are witty, educational, and even inspiring at times. These are great books if you're a patriot, or if you want to be.

Lives of the Noble Grecians and Romans Vol. I—Plutarch

I first learned of Plutarch from Louis L'Amour; his characters often quote him.

Comrade J—Pete Early

Think that hostilities between the US and Russia ended with the close of the Cold War? Think again. This biography of a high-value Russian defector will keep you in suspense and leave you with a new comprehension of what's going on in the world today.

Signature in the Cell—Stephen C. Meyers

Meyers makes a case for the theory of Intelligent Design. Is it possible that generations of middle school biology teachers have been entirely wrong about the origin of life? You might think so if you read this book.

On Liberty—John Stuart Mill

This is a tiny book that has much to say about the philosophy behind free society.

Total Money Makeover—**Dave Ramsey**

I don't like to listen to Dave Ramsey on the radio while I'm in line at Starbucks. I think he's a killjoy. Someday, when I've disciplined my spending habits, I'll be able to give you an excellent recommendation for this book.

How to Learn Any Language—**Barry Farber**

Farber's book gives you a practical method for learning languages.

The Socratic Dialogue's and *The Republic*—**Plato**

Knowing that people consider Plato to be one of history's foremost thinkers, I always shied away from reading his books. Upon reading *The Republic*, I was struck, not by the book's incomprehensible genius, but by its simplicity. Plato's insights are extraordinary, but his language is quite ordinary.

Things That Matter—**Charles Krauthammer**

It's fun to read the work of a modern-day political genius who isn't a raging liberal.

The 80/20 Principle—**Richard Koch**

Koch makes that case for the principle that 20% of what you do will give you 80% of your results. 80% of what we do yields 20%. That simple principle will make you take a long look at how you order your time and resources.

My Book Recommendations

Good to Great—Jim Collins
This book isn't good... It's GR-R-REAT!!! Sorry. That's probably copyrighted. Collins's book is getting old, written in 2001, but it is still at the forefront of leadership training. I want to be a level-5 leader.

The Power of Habit—Charles Duhigg
The Rational Bible—Dennis Prager
The God Who is There—Francis Schaefer
Celebration of Discipline—Richard Foster
Mere Christianity—C.S. Lewis
Orthodoxy—G.K. Chesterton
7 Men and *7 Women*—Eric Metaxas
Taking God at His Word—Kevin DeYoung
Erasing Hell—Francis Chan

Books that inspire

Alexander of Macedon—Harold Lamb
Lamb's beautiful biography of the life of Alexander the Great both inspired and forewarned me. His ascension to the throne at twenty years old challenged me to do more. I have been the pastor of a small church in Westport, Indiana, for ten years. I took on that challenge, at least in part, because of this book. How could one man, so young, do so much? The book also served as a warning against growing too confident or rejecting the counsel of my peers. Lamb's history reads like fiction. I only wish he had written more.

Crusade in Europe—Dwight D. Eisenhower

Eisenhower was appointed as the Supreme Allied Commander in Europe during WWII. He was tasked with building a coalition of nations to liberate Europe from the Axis powers. Eisenhower chronicled his experiences in this autobiography. Eisenhower writes, "My first job was to collect and organize a working team." That was no small thing. Eisenhower said of the task, "History testifies to the ineptitude of coalitions and waging war." And again he states, "Time and again during the summer old army friends warned me that the conception of Allied unity which we took as the foundation of our command scheme was impracticable and impossible... But more than counterbalancing such doleful prophecy was a daily and noticeable growth of cooperation, comradeship, faith, and optimism... "

How was he able to do what had never been done in history, and certainly not to the scale of the Allied forces during WWII? This book is a great place to start in finding the answer to that question.

Escape from Corregidor—Edgar D. Whitcomb

Whitcomb was captured by the Japanese when the island of Corregidor fell during WWII. He escaped, was recaptured, escaped, was caught again, and escaped a final time to tell the tale. This is a white-knuckle page-turner.

My Book Recommendations

Hannibal—Harold Lamb

Reading this book would eventually inspire me to travel to Tunisia as I mentioned in the chapter, "How to Learn."

They Came to Save Us—Larry Arrowood

In this, my favorite of his many books, my dad tells the story of growing up in Appalachia, Kentucky. It's hard to believe that in the middle of the twentieth century his family had no roads or running water. It was a place of poverty, illiteracy, and violence. *Bloody Breathitt* by T.R.C. Hutton chronicles the savagery in great detail. Arrowood's historical fiction takes you to the muddy banks of the North Fork of the Kentucky River for a look at a world as foreign to most of us as the other side of the globe.

Jack Hinson's One Man War—Tom C. Mckinney

Some men need to be left alone. Jack Hinson was just such a man. The North paid a high price for declaring war on this peace-loving neutral.

Up From Slavery—Booker T Washington

Every person that finds themselves under challenging circumstances needs to read this book. Washington touts taking personal responsibility as the means to a better life.

American Pharoah—Joe Drape

I was particularly intrigued by the part that Frances Relihan played in discovering the talents of the horse that would win the American Triple Crown and the Breeders' Cup Classic in 2015. She saw something early on that no one else saw.

The Case for Democracy—**Nathan Sharansky**
Sharansky shares the brutal details of life for a Jew living in Communist Russia. This book made me proud to be an American and thankful for the freedoms we enjoy. Don't think America is exceptional? This book will likely enlighten you.

Unashamed—**Francine Rivers**
Rivers's book was probably written with women in mind. However, I think it is a must-read for anyone dealing with personal shame or trying to understand someone else who is.

The Circle Maker—**Mark Batterson**
It took me a bit to finish this book because I was too busy praying circles around the miracles that I believed God had for me. Nor was it empty enthusiasm. God answered the faith that this book inspired with miracles that are still unfolding five years later.

Never Binge Again—**Glenn Livingston**
This book has a simple and powerful message: commit and stick to it. It reignited my passion for maintaining a healthy weight.

The Greatest Salesman in the World—**Og Mandino**
As a teenager, my parents gave me this book. It helped me

through some of the hardest times of my life.

Aquariums of Pyongyang—**Kang Chol-Hwan**
The Wright Brothers—**David McCullough**
One Nation—**Dr. Ben Carson**
Born Again—**Chuck Colson**
Crazy Love—**Francis Chan**
Born to Run—**Christopher McDougall**
Finding Ultra—**Rich Roll**

Books that will make you want to be better

We Were Soldiers Once and Young—**Harold Moore**
Hal Moore was a man's man. He was first on the ground leading his men into conflict in Vietnam, and he was the last man to get on the chopper when they left. His selfless valor made me want to fight harder for the things I value. Also, I found myself inspired by his wife's efforts to ease the pain of the women who had lost their husbands in the war.

The Frontiersman—**Allan Eckert**
I grew up in Kenton, Ohio and never knew anything about the man whose name the community bares. Simon Kenton was like something out of an Arthur Conan Doyle novel. He was powerful, quick, violent, and principled. He saved the life of Daniel Boone, braved the gauntlet several times, helped to tame the frontier, and lived to be an old man.

Schindler's Ark—**Thomas Keneally**

Schindler was not an entirely moral man. However, the risks that he took and the sacrifices he made to spare the lives of Jews from Nazi tyranny make me feel weak and cowardly.

The Great Siege 1565—**Ernle Bradford**

I read it. I reread it, and again, and again. Bradford's true story of the Knights of Malta is epic. This saga possessed me. I had to travel to that tiny island in the middle of the Mediterranean to touch the walls, see what they saw, and pay homage to men who heroically sacrificed their lives for a cause. The image of Lavalette, standing atop the ruined walls of their stronghold, wielding his courage as deftly as his sword, will never be erased.

The Iron Duke—**Richard Holmes**

When have you ever seen a bust of the First Duke of Wellington? And yet, shrines to Napoleon proliferate. Why? Sir Arthur Wellesley is the man who defeated Napoleon, twice. Richard Holmes will make you want to trade in your French miniature—sorry, I couldn't resist—for a memorial to the genius who outwitted the genius. From his rigid personal discipline to his fearless and ethical battlefield practices, Wellesley's life is a monolith of human distinction. It makes me sad that this work is not available on Audible, but it's one of those books that pushed me beyond my limitations, a must read!

My Book Recommendations

***Hudson Taylor's Spiritual Secret*—Gregg Lewis**
Rarely do I challenge the sovereignty of God like I did along the painful journey of this book. Late one night, ejected from my bed, again, by my five-year-old daughter, I lay in her little "princess" bed. I was reading Lewis's account of the death of Taylor's little girl. Through clenched teeth, I cried, "God, please don't make me go through that." The following morning, I couldn't shake my challenge to God's benevolence. "Why would you do that to a man who loves you?" God's response to that prayer remains one of the defining moments of my life.

Alvin C York—**Douglas Mastriano**
The Autobiography of George Mueller—**George Mueller**
Life of Nelson—**Robert Southey**
Life of David Brainerd—**Jonathan Edwards**
The Cost of Discipleship—**Dietrich Bonhoeffer**

Books that will entertain or relax

***The Sackett series, The Walking Drum, Last of the Breed,* or anything else by Louis L'Amour**
I am pretty sure I've read everything L'Amour ever wrote, twice. Some I have read many times over. His writing is simple and straightforward. The good guy wins and gets the girl. The geographical descriptions are vast and transporting. His characters are built from Plutarch's biographies and the Bible. The gun battles are epic, and the fistfight descriptions are the

best I've ever read. The power of L'Amour is that he walked the paths of the western men he describes. These books are clean, entertaining, and not so suspenseful that they'll keep you up at night.

Complete Sherlock Holmes—**Arthur Conan Doyle**
White Fang and *The Sea Wolf*—**Jack London**
Ghost in the Wires—**Kevin Mitnick**
A Captain's Duty—**Richard Philips**
Catch Me If You Can—**Frank Abagnale**
The Eighty-Dollar Champion—**Elizabeth Letts**

Books that disturb

The Gulag Archipelago—**Alexander Solzhenitsyn**
Solzhenitsyn recounts how Communism grew from infancy to maturity in Russia. He experienced the corruption of the Russian legal system and lived through the brutality of the Gulag. Reading *The Gulag Archipelago* is like studying the lifecycle of a plague. His macabre recollections cast an appalling shadow over Communism and its cousin, Socialism.

Jerusalem—**Simon Seabag Montefiore**
I was listening to *Jerusalem* while traveling a winding Indiana backroad. The narrator was recounting the history of the Crusades. When the Christians had the power, they abused the Jews and/or the Muslims. When the Muslims regained the advantage, they committed atrocities upon the Jew and/

or the Christians. If the Jews had the upper hand, they wielded it in reprisals. Back and forth the hatred and violence were passed down through generations. I was overtaken by a sense of rage at all of them. I began pounding the steering wheel and yelling at the top of my lungs, "Nobody is right! It's all nauseating and putrid hate. None of them are serving God." It was a powerful moment in the formation of my attitude about religion and the history of the Christian church. It made me want to return to the dusty streets of Judea, immortalized in the Gospels, to find a Savior who yielded to crucifixion in innocence saying, "Father, forgive them."

The Chris Farley Show—Tanner Colby and Tom Farley

Chris Farley's speech to a group of recovering addicts reveals the way that he honestly felt about drugs and alcohol. No one will laugh as they hear his impassioned pleas for the men to get away from that junk. It hurts to know that before he was a self-destructing addict, he was a sincerely kind and religious young man. In a religious college, he was introduced by professing Christians to the world of alcohol. It quickly took control of his life and never relinquished that hold. This book makes me question why any responsible Christian leader would ever use the power of their office to promote alcohol. It is indeed a shame, and the tragedies are so unnecessary.

Anna Karenina—Leo Tolstoy

Tolstoy made me hate Anna. I became enraged at her in the early chapters and wished the worst for her throughout the whole journey. The landscape of this book is prodigious. The characters are so numerous that I finished the last chapter still not knowing who some of the people were. Along the way, Tolstoy navigates the intricacies of beauty, manliness, marriage, hunting, art, husbandry, and many other areas of life with professorial dexterity. The conclusion is long in coming but beyond worth the suspense.

Tamerlane—Harold Lamb

Sometimes the truth is undesirable for its disillusioning qualities. If ignorance is bliss, truth can be agonizing. It's hard to face the realities of what our forbearers were doing as they established the towpath we're still following. It challenges us to comply with a bit less blindness. The world Lamb reveals surrounding the saga of *Tamerlane* is eye-opening. Like Montefiore's *Jerusalem*, it makes you want to return to source materials for faith. There are no pending tell-alls that threaten to expose Christ.

CONCLUSION

A Final Thought

In the months that have passed from beginning this work to seeing its publication, I've read a few amazing books that have altered my perspectives yet again. So much so, that as I write these final words, I'm tempted to go back to page one and start all over. However, I'm going to do something more worthwhile; I'm going to find some more great books and read them instead.

I hope that as you set this book down, you, too, go in search of another, and let this be the beginning of your great relationship with reading.

References for the recommended reading list.

- **Ernest Shackleton**—(https://www.bbc.com/news/magazine-35633374)

- **Bruce Lee**—(https://houseofbrucelee.blogspot.com/search/label/BOOKS)

- **Steve Jobs**—(https://www.inc.com/geoffrey-james/12-books-steve-jobs-wanted-you-to-read.html)

- **Ivanka Trump— https://www.amazonbookreview.com/post/f5a3d816-f8ee-4ce1-bd8e-73e390034b46/celebrity-picks-ivanka-trumps-favorite-reads-of-2017**

- **Elon Musk**—(https://www.cnbc.com/2018/05/24/50-books-that-inspire-elon-musk-jeff-bezos-and-other-tech-titans.html)

- **Jeff Bezos**—(https://www.cnbc.com/2018/05/24/50-books-that-inspire-elon-musk-jeff-bezos-and-other-tech-titans.html)

- **Meghan Markle**—(http://www.meghansmirror.com/meghan-markle-book/)

- **George S. Patton**—(*The Leader's* Bookshelf— Adm. James Stavridis USN (Ret.), R. Manning Ancell)

- **Louis L'Amour**—(*Education of a Wandering Man*—Louis L'Amour)

- **Henry David Thoreau**— https://www. amazon.com/gp/product/0520063465/ ref=as_li_tl?imprToken=SICnqI1H3SCJQiQzs8 nLBw&slotNum=0&ie=UTF8&camp=1789&c reative=390957&creativeASIN=0520063465&li nkCode=w61&tag=stucosuccess-20&linkId=Y-UDWNAWRAVQALY5Q

- **Abraham Lincoln**— https://quod.lib.umich. edu/j/jala/2629860.0028.204/--what-abraham-lincoln-readan-evaluative-and-annotated-list?rgn=main;view=fulltext

- **Theodore Roosevelt**—(*Theodore Rex*—Edmund Morris)

- **Bill Gates**—(http://www.Gatesnotes.com)

- **George W. Bush**— https://www. amazonbookreview.com/post/7c810951-b626-4dcd-9d73-7d25bea1c889/george-w-bushsreading-list

- **Pope Francis**— http://favobooks.com/
  politicians/129-Pope-Francis-books-spiritually-
  enriching.html

- Martin Luther King Jr.— http://favobooks.
  com/politicians/125-Luther-King-powerful-
  books-that-shaped-his-personality.html